Mystic Land
and Celtic Saints

Other Books by Ronnie Smith

The Last White Ruby

The Royal Princess and the Three Magical Gifts

Roses for the Most High:
Poetry Celebrating the Mystical Christian Path

The Sky is for Wonder

Deployed Flight and Sometimes Eternity

Mystic Land
and Celtic Saints

RONNIE SMITH

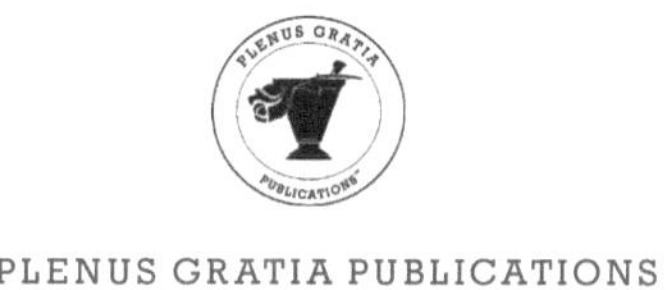

PLENUS GRATIA PUBLICATIONS

Ronnie Smith/Plenus Gratia Publications®
PlenusGratiaToday@gmail.com

Book Cover & Interior Design by The Book Cover Whisperer:
OpenBookDesign.biz

Mystic Land and Celtic Saints/Ronnie Smith. —1st ed.

978-0-9980465-9-4 Paperback
978-1-7356595-1-0 Hardcover
978-1-7356595-0-3 eBook

FIRST EDITION

This book is dedicated
to the
Blessed Mother Mary

Contents

Acknowledgments

I would like to express special thanks and appreciation to the people who have encouraged me and helped make this book come to fruition. Works do not manifest through unsupported inspiration of the artist, and therefore those who offered assistance, faith, friendship, and professionalism are dearly appreciated and remembered here: Kathleen Sweeney, Edward Sellner, Dorothy Wilder, Dara Molloy, Mindie and Daniel Burgoyne, Terry Grotpeter, Don Jordan, and Megan Burkhart.

The poems *Saint Baya and Saint Maura, The Utterance of Baile Shear,* and *Gougane Barra and Saint Finbarr* first appeared in **Leaping Clear Magazine**.

Saint Modomnoc first appeared in **Tiny Seed Journal**.

The Monastic first appeared in **Roses for the Most High, Celebrating the Mystical Christian Path.**

All interior illustrations were created by Ronnie Smith and are available in individual giclee prints by contacting the artist at: plenusgratiatoday@gmail.com.

Foreword

In order to produce this wonderful collection of poetry, Ronnie Smith had to step into the bath, and immerse himself completely in the Celtic spiritual tradition.

With commitment, perseverance, steadfastness and the investment of a lot of time and money, he visited all the places, and encountered the echoed presence of the great saints in their own habitat.

Most people who write about this heritage do so from a left-brain perspective. That is, they research the historical data and then give us their analysis.

Ronnie, on the other hand, approaches the subject in the same way that the monks in their scriptoria approached the texts of scripture. These monks absorbed the text—possibly with their left brain—and then re-expressed it through their right-brain in the form of art and images.

Ronnie's right-brain approach has produced a wonderful collection of poetry (as well as some art) that captures the essence of these saints and places.

These poems will take the reader into the heart of Celtic spirituality—where the divine presence is found in nature. Every tree, every animal, every place of beauty is a gateway to the divine and a manifestation of the sacred.

The Celtic saints were mystics, as indeed is Ronnie. They sought first and foremost an experience of the divine. They were not so concerned with the heady theologizing of those in Rome and on continental Europe.

Choosing to live in places of wilderness and beauty, these mystics immersed themselves in an experience of wonder. Travelling as *peregrinati* across land and sea, they sought direction from angels, and believed they would be shown their 'place of resurrection'.

Ronnie captures this sense of mystical journeying, of finding the presence of the divine everywhere. His poetry is itself a mystical experience. Through his poetry, we too become *peregrinati*, visiting the places once trodden by these Celtic saints and seeing these places through their eyes.

Dara Ó Maoildhia / Dara Molloy
Inis Mor, Aran Islands, September 2021

Introduction

Over the course of my life I traveled much as an athlete and aviator. This travel led to the insular Celtic regions in Ireland and the United Kingdom, France, and Spain. Interest in the cultures and histories followed. I wanted to visit these countries on my own. While writing a poetry book about the mystic saints of the Christian church, I visited Ireland to see what it offered that rich heritage. After visiting Ireland with the group, "Thin Places Tours" with Mindie Burgoyne, I realized that the Celtic lands of Ireland, the UK, Brittany, and Galicia were so abundant with saints that they deserved a book of their own.

Many of these saints I encountered on this tour hailed from the Golden Age of the Saints, from the 4th through the 9th centuries. They were the initial missionaries to Cork, Donegal, and all places in between and abroad. It amazed me how they did it. And their zeal and faith astounded me. Thus started this journey.

I began to read about the saints and plan more trips to Ireland, the UK, and Brittany. Inspiration from reading about their lives flowed into poetry. Shortly into this unraveling adventure, I started receiving dreams while asleep and visions during meditation that guided and encouraged me along the way. Most of my adult life I have had these intuitive perceptions from time to time, though I struggled to understand why.

For instance, on the occasion in 2012 just before departing for the Catholic pilgrimage at Lourdes, France, during meditation I had a vision of a man who greeted me in a white tunic. I telepathically asked him why he was showing up in my meditation and what was he doing putting things in order all around me. He said, "My name is Luke, and I'm going to heal and help you in Lourdes." I thanked him and thought, "What a nice chap!" Three days into the pilgrimage, I ran into a glass wall and almost knocked myself out. A day later, still concussed, I attended mass, and there outside the doorway was a tall white statue of Saint Luke the Apostle. Then the realization of the vision hit me, followed by deep gratitude.

Moving forward to this keen interest in the Celtic isles, in 2016 a lucid, vivid dream found me watching two monks carry the relics of Saint Andrew ashore to the land of the Picts (present day Scotland). This actually happened in the 8th century in the time of the Irish Abbott Tuathal at the monastery at Rigmond. I was lifted upward in the dream until I could view the entirety of the Celtic Isles.

The famous and holy Cross of Saint Andrew was superimposed, overlaying all the isles. A voice then spoke to me saying, "This will be your mission. Put all your heart into writing this book that you have started and you will be given everything you need. With all that you have, bring the life and spirit, beauty and truth, of the Celtic Saints to the world and go forward with confidence because you have the blessing of the holy Saint Andrew."

A number of people looked at me in a strange way when I began telling them I was traveling to Ireland and Scotland

and other Celtic destinations to write a poetry book on the land and its saints.

On the other hand, every military G.I. has familiarity with taskings and missions. I was assigned many in my years in the Air Force. But who saw this one coming? To be faithful to what I thought God wanted of me, I in earnest started planning further excursions to the Celtic Isles, kept reading more books about the lives of the saints, and researched that age of exemplary flourishing of Christendom. As the inspiration dictated, I began painting illustrations for the various sections and saints of the book. I was initially drawn to St. Finbar, St. Gobnait, St. Columba, Sts. Aidan and Cuthbert, and the great Saint Brigit. The more saints I discovered, the more I realized profound gratefulness for this journey.

So, to access these countries firsthand was to try to encounter the paths of the saints and to get a sense of the land. The period of the golden age of Christendom in the Celtic Isles is roughly 400-800 A.D. This is the era which this book covers. It is bookended by two powerfully dynamic events on the stage of human civilization: the departure of the Roman legions from Britain in about 410, and the arrival of the Vikings in the late 700's. The Viking massacre on Lindisfarne in 793 and the slaughter of 68 monks at the Iona Monastery in 806 were emphatically defining.

As much as these saints were models of Christian simplicity and holiness, they also experienced God through intimate contact with the elements of nature. This was a heritage that flowed from the pre-Christian Celts, which held a holy closeness to the natural world through their "nature religion". An outstanding feature of the Druidic-based spirituality was living life as an integral part of the environment, communing with God through all of their daily activities. The idea of Man vs. Environment was not as pronounced as the union derived from living as an actor in and with the environment.

To get a sense of this culture of union with Mother Earth, I studied Alexander Carmichael's stalwart work, "Carmina Gadelica" (Songs/Amulets of the Gaels). He collected and published the poems, prayers, chants, incantations, and songs of the Celtic folk culture in the Scottish Gaelic Highlands and Islands that was dying out in the late 1800s. This collection calls to account the recognition of God and the spiritual Kingdom of Souls, as participants with us in every act of life, from waking in the morning to making the bed, milking the cows, and setting sail to fish the sea. An example is the "Rune of the Well" which a young woman would sing on her way in the evening light to get water from the well:

> The shelter of Mary Mother
> Be nigh my hands and my feet
> To go out to the well
> And to bring me safely home
> And to bring me safely home
>
> May warrior Michael aid me
> May Brigit calm preserve me
> May sweet Brianna give me light
> And Mary pure be near me
> And Mary pure be near me

In essence, these cultural writings attest to an agrarian

society of unassuming people, and so their saints. For these saints of the Celtic Golden Age (4ᵗʰ-9ᵗʰ C.) were without all the distractions of hi-tech today. They invoked God's presence, the saints and angels of the celestial world, into their daily labors. And those labors were of simple intent: work hard all summer, all day long, to be able to survive the winter. Their food came from the hand of God. The safety of their journey was in God's hands. Fair weather was divine blessing. There was much to be grateful for. These are spiritual truths for anyone in any age. Why? Because it teaches one to bless God for everything. For the good and the so-called bad.

In the first section, this book expounds upon this co-habitable vision of the kingdom of the physical world. The inherent divinity present and active through its parallel (to the human) angelic hierarchy and sub-hierarchies, is involved in Creation through the mineral, plant, and animal kingdoms. These realms are dependent upon, not subservient to, the human kingdom. The second section of the book entails the poetic and intuitive narrative of the lives of the saints.

The secrets of Creation lie in the sacred heart of the Creator, The All, The Good and The Beauty. The mystical path was sought by these Celtic men and women of devotional fervor. Their devotion and idealism were the hallmarks of the Celtic Golden Age. Learning about, intuiting, and to an extent experiencing their work, I have been caressed by waves of grace. I feel mentored by their deeds and celestial provocations. As they sowed the sea lanes of the Inner and Outer Hebrides with the gospel in their hand-hewn currachs, my own at times rowed soul-swept through their mystical sea that lapped my shore. And just as mysteriously I found the blessings of the Celtic saints. As their path of devotion led to higher callings, so did mine, in sight of Mother Mary. This book is a pilgrimage through the Celtic lands and the lives of its saints. A pilgrimage, I must humbly assess at times, into the chartless recesses of God.

The Mystic Land

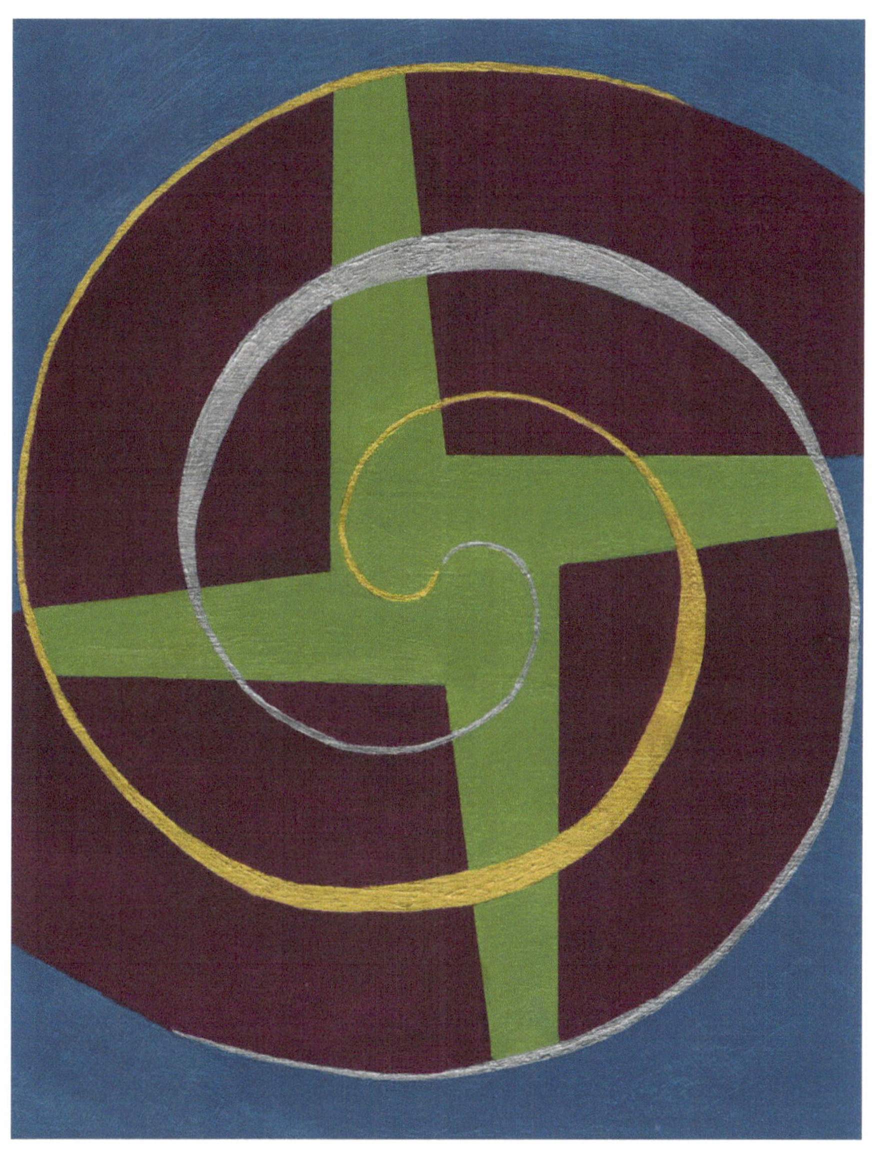

THE TEACHER OF ANGELS AND MEN

The sanguine-red color of sacrifice (of the ego) is the foundation for the evolution of religion. Saint Brigit's cross of Christianity evokes the spiral of growth of human (gold) and angelic (silver) realms intertwined in God's plan on Earth, the living green of the cross.

Skellig Michael

This Rock of Saint Michael, the mists surround
The spire of ascetics in shroud has drowned
The salt-spray of memories scrubbed them clean
Mysterious storms left the sea serene
Basilica praised the Eternal crowned

This skellig of Michael can wail and hound
As wounds of the ego through flesh expound
For saints chiseled steps that would tread the soul
As ritual hardens a gem from coal
Basilica praised the Eternal crowned

This skellig of Michael, its peaks have wound
From necklace of foam's everlasting sound
Its sandstone will sparkle with rain-rich green
Yet battled its saints like a beached Marine
Basilica praised the Eternal crowned

This Rock of Saint Michael, my hallowed ground
The brine of its stars, to that lair I'm bound
Afloat in a limitless sky patrol
To navigate night by celestial pole
Basilica praised the Eternal crowned

Skellig Michael is also known as Great Skellig; The Rock of St Michael; Sceilg Mhichíl; Sgeillic; Inis-scgellge. It is a splinter of two peaks that rise hundreds of feet above the Atlantic Ocean, seven miles off the shores of County Kerry, Ireland. Sceilg Mhichíl illustrates, as no other property can, the extremes of a Christian monasticism characterizing much of North Africa, the Near East and Europe. The monastery, its cells and oratories, stand as monuments to the faith of Celtic culture in the divine protection of Saint Michael the Archangel.[1]

---

1   UNESCO World Heritage, *Sceilg Mhichil*, https://whc.unesco.org/en/list/757/ License CC-BY-SA IGO 3.0, 1996 (modified from original).

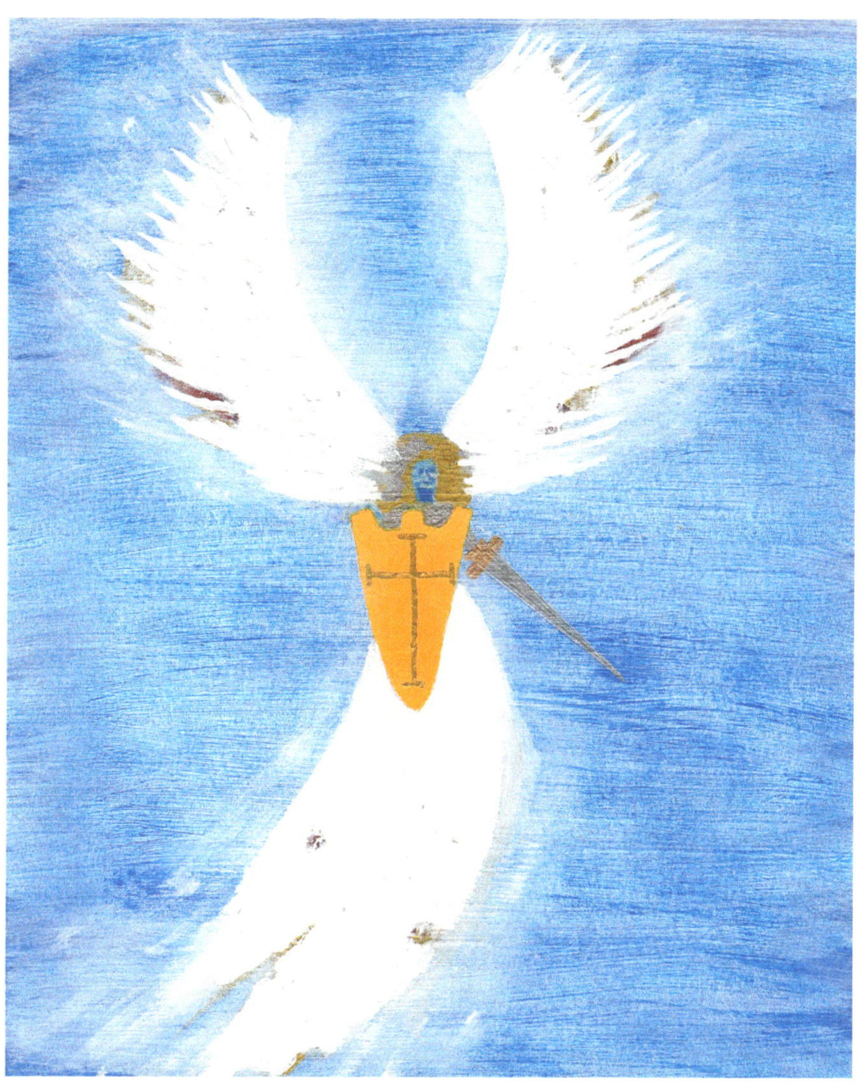

SAINT MICHAEL THE GREAT ARCHANGEL

After conversion to Christianity, the lore and testament of the Celts held a solid connection to Saint Michael the Archangel. He was, among other roles, seen as the protector of the Celt tribes over land and sea. It is no surprise then that we see his dedicated provenance at the great promontories of Skellig Michael off the coast of Kerry, Mont-Saint-Michel, Brittany and Saint Michael's Mount, Cornwall.

Highland Light

A salmon sunrise wildly leaps
a-thrash in streams that teem my heart

> Whoever You—your zephyr plays
> to fondle this created world

> Whoever You—your sky that frays
> shall scallop clouds, flotilla pearled

> Whoever You—your seagulls graze
> the wave that Fibonacci curled

> Whoever You—your lunar rays
> shall paint the darkness they have hurled

When clouds diffuse the light and You
Make vistas pant delight and You
Fill seas that foam with dream and You
Then sing through everything and You

Send thunder with the Mother's rain
To flood the throats that swill her flow
And meteors that stained terrain
Like dollops topping green gateau

In traditional Scottish geography, the **Highlands** refer to that part of Scotland north-west of the Highland Boundary Fault, which crosses mainland Scotland in a near-straight line from Helensburgh to Stonehaven.[2]

2 *Highlands / Region, Scotland, United Kingdom*, Encyclopedia Britannica, Accessed June 1, 2020.

Seven Sanctuaries of Inis Cealtra

When first we drummed the lough, with numbers swelling
numbers swelling
the saints to pines of tall desire came felling
Invasion wrought seclusion from the towns
lest life so unfulfilled by raving drowns
and holy wells might echo churches knelling

A tower's cell would foist the sins expelling
Annexed to graveyards with their vain foretelling
And altars, pilgrims venerate by rounds
. . . when first we drummed the lough

From village square to farms where God was dwelling
I felt Saint Caiman's cloud of prayer compelling
as anchorites by grace atone their grounds
For Viking fleets could not defeat these crowns
of Christ's red cross in solitude excelling
. . . when first we drummed the lough

Inis Cealtra (inish-keltra) means 'holy island' in Irish. It is located off the west shore of Lough Derg in Ireland. It was once a monastic hermitage and thriving monastic center. The Vikings ravaged and sacked it twice. It was repopulated both times and served the religious community until the Reformation. High King Brian Boru, the final liberator of Ireland from the Vikings, contributed a church and round tower to the island.[3]

3   Wikipedia contributors, *Inis Cealtra*, Wikipedia, The Free Encyclopedia, Accessed January 20, 2020.

Holy Island of Lindisfarne

This sea of clouds still sweeps the sky and floods
across the sun

This island lured Iona with the wiles of one lost foal
The rhythm of the tide extolled The Way of
monk and nun

Because the call of Christians is a game of one-on-one
Saint Aidan found this place of harbor more
than an atoll
This sea of clouds still sweeps the sky and floods
across the sun

Before the Age of Vikings when the savagery was done
This island was a refuge like the Christ within the soul
The rhythm of the tide extolled The Way of
monk and nun

The land was just a fragment of the magic just begun
When Cuthbert cracked the gate and walked as
shepherd on patrol
This sea of clouds still sweeps the sky and floods
across the sun

The passion of the Gospels lit the poetry of Donne
This island bore a light with an illuminated scroll

The rhythm of the tide extolled The Way of
monk and nun

The road of holiness is still a path for anyone
Our inner island is a haven where we find the soul
Its sea of clouds still sweeps the sky and floods
across the sun
And rhythm of the tide extols The Way of
monk and nun

Lindisfarne, a tidal island in northeast England, became
a center in monastic Christendom when King St. Oswald
sought from Iona Monastery a priest and company to evan-
gelize his kingdom of Northumbria. Iona on the west coast
sent one Bishop Saint Aidan, who with his group of priests
and monks set up the monastery presence at Lindisfarne
that paved the way for the great golden age of Northern
Britain's Christianity.[4]

4   Haswell-Smith, Hamish, *The Scottish Islands*, Edin-
burgh, Canongate ©2004.

The Utterance of Baile Shear

Here was a foam-white pup, born of a gray seal
getting all grown up on mother's thick milk
nodding into naps at low tide on a seaweed bed
combing the sea back into itself without thinking

Miles of blond sand salt the winds and waves
sifting the sea back into itself without thinking
formed by this holy three—Wind, Sand, and Wave
wingbeats above fanning, then gliding the invisible

Rain columns pillar their dark cloud mansion
Halos of sunlight arouse this sculpted sky
pouring the sea back into itself without thinking
widening the mouth of history's swallowed things

Here stood a soul, blown by God to this coast
the walk of peeking sandbars where
footprints disappear
caressing endless surf that one day laps the sun
yawning the sea back into itself without thinking

I visited **Baile Shear** and Scotland's Outer Hebrides to encounter the areas where the Celtic saints explored and taught on their missionary journeys. I was quite alone on this miles-long beach on the western coast of the island. I could see deep gray rainclouds form a hedgerow in the sky to the south over the water. The sun was hovering above it in its entirety sending spears of light through it. From the cloud-bank, rain shafts were pouring into the sea like columns. At the same time the flat sea-soaked strand upon which I stood was glazed like a mirror. I saw within this looking glass a surreal depiction of the natural elements in the sky. The waves rolled rhythmically in long white ropes of foam as they crashed one after the other on a sand bank further offshore. Seagulls wheeled and terns strutted the banks. I prayed to God for the understanding of our brethren who long ago lived with almost nothing materially, but who lived for the divine idea of an ultimate union with God. In this revelatory moment I experienced it. It was given to me. Here, the Creator, with a wisdom too complex to comprehend in its infinity, allowed me to connect to the harmony of every force of nature acting individually yet as One. Experiencing this innate divinity, its ecstasy lasted for hours.

Baile Shear (bal-la sheer) or Baleshare means "east town" in Scottish Gaelic. It is a tidal flat island off the west coast of North Uist (yoost), Outer Hebrides.[5]

5   Haswell-Smith, Hamish, *The Scottish Islands*, Edinburgh, Canongate 2004.

Hermits at the Edge of the World

As the crest of that Christendom caromed the edge
of the world
Be it known that the bugles of archangels
muzzled the din
Let its pitch have no rest like a bagpipe whose breath
ever skirled
Even though a sea odyssey purges the demons and sin
Seven nights at full sail toward the light, there my
search shall begin
So my currach's sweet stroke glides a current to life
deep within

Saint Columba enraptured his monks to the beauty
that swirled
And on each of the islands a hermitage cell was an inn
It was stone and not stilts that was stacked, not the pine
that was knurled
Nor a matter of shelter in boats sealed with animal skin
And twelve nights at full sail toward the light, there my
search shall begin
My own currach's sweet stroke glides a current to life
deep within

Just as every sweet flight into union with God
had unfurled

I launched out with the heart to make prayer take the
fight for the win
The Lord's battle-dressed knight yanked the noose from
the knot I had twirled
I look out and then in to forego my cantankerous twin
Forty nights at full sail toward the light, there my search
shall begin
Let my currach's sweet stroke glide a current to life
deep within

I was blown by the stars to the islands the
continents hurled
Spying all these great lights I would navigate
dots of a pin
Hence the monks of Iona found waters the arctic
had purled
As the cold of a netherworld's riptides had ice-
pools that spin
Every night at full sail toward the light, there my search
shall begin
Let my currach's sweet stroke glide a current to life
deep within

The **currach** was the standard seafaring boat used by the
Celts on the sea road between the Outer and Inner Hebrides,
Ireland, and Britain.[6]

____

6   Marsden, John, *Sea-Road of the Saints*, Edinburgh,
Floris Books, 1995.

The Sainthood of Trees

The trees are seeding
and shedding what they need no more
What they do when light retreats
When we all in the whorl of winter
can sow a hole from which to grow
with the light that promises return

And for now, deepening
into each other like the trees
Who, fading from their hey-day
slowly loosen well-worn bark
by the swinging pendulum of seasons

The wisdom of a tree
will bless us by a life of purpose
Its vibrant exaltation of the One Life

The inimitable Ecstasy that spreads its arms
to sky and to all winged beings
mortal and immortal

The inimitable Ecstasy profounding life
awakening life, brewing life
harboring little lives
leaving traces upon life

There is mystery in your hidden rings
and subterranean roots
Those neural tendrils that bind a family
of living forest to holy Earth

That that knows no desperation for another
always knows and always has known
its purpose boring lightless depth

To blossom above ground in glory
seeming to nod, unnoticed
seeming to honor perpetual union

That that you do in silence before all others

God-Immanent in all living things of nature was at the core of the Celtic religio-spiritual ethos.

The Thin Place

I subsist on the breath from your voice

Of the barrens, who bend with tenderness
to nuzzle the newborn to life

Of the river's silver grail
that empties the sun into forest

Of the raincloud's greatest psalm
retelling its mystery to meadow

Of the wells, whose tranquil tones
arrange a chamber for angels

Of the stones, who tremored from giants
who in mist disappeared with the ice

Of the trees, who twist me like wizards
and wither a thousand years

Mystical Sphere

O Angel of Earth
when the sky would plunder rainbow's blue
You tamed the White Light
to let turquoise splash across the butterfly's wing

O Angel of Earth
when the seas bubbled, seethed, and cooled
You tamed the White Light
to send flapping and crawling the flaunting myriads

O Angel of Earth
when the ages of fire consumed the world
You tamed the White Light
to let lava drool the footstool of God

O Angel of Earth
when the waters roared, then grayed and shimmered
You tamed the White Light
to send gilded lightning coursing through ore

O Angel of Earth
when the winds breathed and whirled from birth
You tamed the White Light
to let mountains whistle their endless longing

O Angel of Earth
when the spirits of ice laid crowns on your orb

You tamed the White Light
to send icebergs to blaze the blinding seas

Great Stones

Ancient caves paint tales of light
rhythm stroked gray stone
sacred wheels evoked the sun
Fire's constant flight

Shovels filled with chalk and sod
would before gray stone
trench and groom for gathering ton
—glaciers left their god

Angels of the sky have blown
clouds to form gray stone
Hence the henge may ever run
mystic plane to throne

Watching sunset's fire ball
melting o'er gray stone
land and sky ally as One
sown to till the All

The **great standing stone** circles in the Celtic Isles, and across northern Europe for that matter, have been linked to astronomical, mathematical, geographical, and spiritual concepts, where ceremonies would have been held with a focus on an ancestral religion, celestial bodies, and the dead. Scientific excavation continues. These often dramatic stone formations defy our modern world with a sheer veil into an ancient Neolithic era 5,000 years ago.

Maire's Grail

Her radiant verses flower
the twines of the harp that part the Gaelic mist

Reviving the scent of sojourns
that ghost becalmed lands dew-wet with soul song

Whose sea breeze intrudes
salting with banshee callings a saga my heart cannot forget

Raised from the mounds on the grange
to braid the heroic road ahead with vistas left behind

I was greatly blessed to see a solo performance of **Maire Brennan** in the early 2000s in Arlington, Virginia. Her gift evoked such a powerful reconnection inside me to the Celtic/Gaelic culture as to inspire the above poem. From the ancient bards to the present writings of Gaelic poets and musicians, artistic compositions have indelibly evoked the connection of the people to the soul of the mystical landscape. A number of modern, new age, and folk artists have contributed to this legacy.

Croagh Patrick, The Holy Mountain

Thousands of years before empire emerged, they came
to hunt, to gather, to huddle the coast and cook the fish
They wrote upon rocks and painted divinity on
ritual ponds
They built a fort to crown a king, a scion for your peak
From flint to bronze, they'd scurry your raw
skirts, cut wool
and devise wonders to order mountain, sun,
moon, and star

The stones they'd align to count the suns that
splash humanity
They moved like percussion to the notes of the
pitch of light
hiking your meadow, trudging your bog, ascending
your shadow
To the Hill of the Eagle did they

They came for peace and promise offered by
dawn and dusk
They are left standing as megaliths on your olive-
tawny carpet
They are left lying in your barrows, cairns clattered high
They are left animating legends birthed before
Time restarted

and Patrick called children to his church of
the Man-God

They came to your sanctified fields that garden Creation
with a gospel whose bible concludes your singular Zion
But temples were driven, like an abbey tower, to ruin
An oratory entombed, stone still upon stone,
telling ghosted
roads about famine extolled under the zeal of trolls

I was an ox grazing waves of your vale, plowed
by the wind
You transplant us by your slope of
insurmountable symmetry
guiding the sun like a ball rolling into the
sleeve of loughs
and hollows, where clouds play but can't hide

O! How they clasp you with their misty cloak!

For in faith they came—and still we come—from West
and East, at least to meet Tranquility, seasons
traveling through
us like membranes for your rain-worn fold, its trickling
flute flowing with ten trillion tears since Christ

I arrived at the base of **Croagh Patrick** on a mild day. I hiked for two-hours to reach the summit where elements of St. Patrick's pilgrimages remain along with a modest chapel. A storm blew in and began to grip the upper third of the mountain. I was leaning into the rain and wind as I approached the peak. Nothing was visible beyond 15 feet at the zenith, as if I had entered the Cloud of Unknowing, the mystical terrain of contemplative disciples. Some of our physical excursions through life take on the metaphor of the inner journey of seeking God within oneself, and this time, appropriately, when seeking experiences with God in the external environment. Repeating one's love for the divine providence through prayer or mantra (as I fervently recited in this storm) is a means to awaken to a path within and provide a new perspective of the world without. I knew I needed to hike up this mountain, not knowing why. The only physical refuge at the peak in the storm was the sturdy exterior walls of the chapel. A symbol for the sanctuary, the holy of holies, within us. Herein lies my highest realization of the experience, where physical and spiritual surrender became one.

Croagh Patrick in County Mayo, Ireland is an ancient mountain icon in the landscape. Almost a symmetrical peak from certain vantage points, it was long a place of pilgrimage and a strategic hill fort before the arrival of Christianity. Saint Patrick made it a hermitage retreat and it became a Christian pilgrimage as well.[7]

------

7   *The History of Croagh Patrick from the Croagh Patrick Visitor Centre*, Teach na Missa, www.croagh-patrick.com. Retrieved June 10, 2015.

Saint Morwenna's Morwenstow

Your cliff by the shore is an altar for gull
Whose cries to the waters will mesh into one
As waves over rocks turn to foam on a skull
and wingspans will widen and whiten by sun

Releasing the holy from icons we mull . . .

We pile our worn stones and erect from life's sprawl
a wall for a castle still layered with rain
The bastion of hearts needs no structure at all
The hearth of the soul is its flaming domain

Increasing the holy in icons we mull . . .

When sitting we'll find that the mind becomes full
like knitting the past to be gobbled by moth
Where emptiness strides, it weaves through the wool
unfurling the mantle of Christ for our cloth

The fleece in the holiest icons we mull . . .

Morwenna, I linger in mist like a thrall
where heaven makes known my red sunset of quest
For even your coast becomes clear after squall
that ravens may drink from your spring to the west

Unceasingly holy these icons we mull . . .

Several places are named after **Saint Morwenna**, notably Morwenstow in Cornwall, where her relics are probably buried under the church floor and where she has appeared.[8]

8   Lapa, Dmitry, Orthodox Christianity, *Women Saints of Cornwall*, http://orthochristian.com/114524.html.

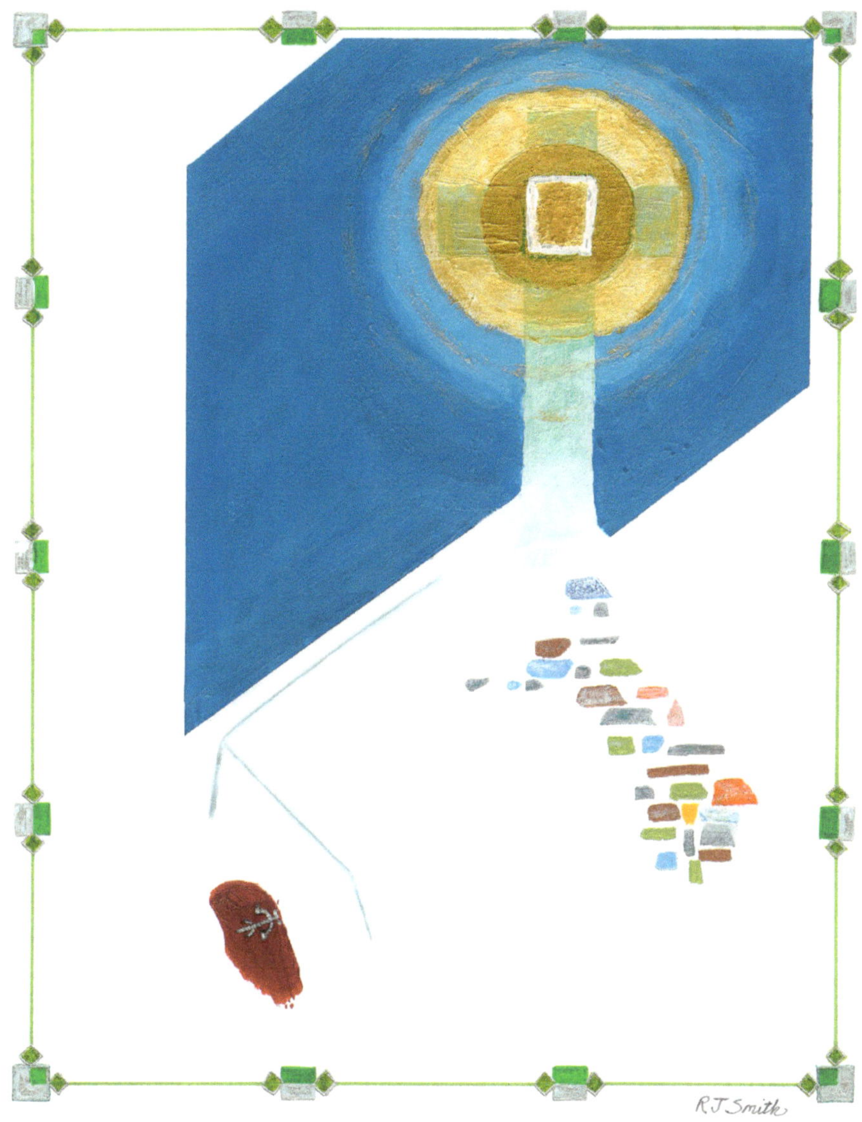

SAINT FINBARR'S ORATORY

Saint Finbarr's missionary work in southern Ireland and elsewhere sent a beacon of Christ's light to all he touched.

Gougane Barra and Saint Finbarr

Before the River Lee circles the Great Island
the faraway hills till a lough of quiet power
where the soul can adjourn the drama
from the stage of itself

Miracle will steep this fine hour
    by the slippings and slaps of water
    by the friction and calm of air
    by dank stone and pigment of bark
in a teakettle of subtleties
whose vapors envelop
my garden of intimacy with God

Without your pilgrimage
without your fast in hollow cell
without the borderlands that either comfort us
or draw us to swig of wild springs that await
the eye will not grasp the woolly clouds
that ascend and descend through lassos of sun
brandishing never-lands blue

For even when fishermen in boats are blown
they heave a net to haul treasure from the sea
And why I followed; because you cast you
to God's silent winds of nothingness and towed

Saint Finbarr (Bairre, Barra, Barr, Fynbarry and Fynd-Barr) was the first Bishop and Patron of Cork. Many miracles were recorded. He established a hermitage in the hills at the head of the River Lee called Gougane Barra. He established a monastery at the site of present-day Cork city. Also took missionary journeys through the Hebrides. His name is held in Scotland in veneration.[9]

---

9 O'Hanlon, Rev. John, *Lives of the Irish Saints*, Dublin, James Duffy and Sons, 1875.

Castles Three

I once was a lord over castles three
and one was like forest growing round me
I starved for the moon
and climbed a great tree
and carved out a house for my supper and tea

I once was a lord over castles three
and one was like water flowing round me
I've swum like a fish
from streams to the sea
and sometimes I'd leap in the hope to be free

I once was a lord over castles three
and one was like whirlwind blowing round me
I jumped into flight
yet I was a flea
and clung onto angels and devils to be

I am now a lord over castles three
and wake to the roosters crowing round me
I rise with a sun
that no one can see
and prize many colors that pageant my glee

The Way of the Owl

Once I, one gleaming night, played lacrosse
with the moon
Beams of brilliance that thrilled are now lost
with the moon!

Sleeping or waking, I can sense my sister owl
Forest minions creep streams never crossed
with the moon

Truth she seeks, not desires that plunder the glitter
Truth and a tree bat an albatross with the moon!

Translucent wings she'll preen. Pristine with no towel!
Beloved, her silence is not tossed to the moon!

She sweeps dim forest as a candid transmitter
Luminous with the light that she flossed with the moon

On lofty alps of the soul, the listening prowl
And she shall know her way when it's glossed
by the moon!

Mute in flight, I shall have talons of a critter
To then clench the dark world when embossed
by the moon!

The Celtic Christians believed a part of God dwells in a sacred way in all things, inherited from their druidic predecessors. The **Owl** was but one sacred animal which represented divine attributes of the Creator. For the mystic, this was clear in the meditative nature of this bird.

The Ogham Song (The Alphabet of Trees)

T From birth, The Pristine speaks dialects of Birch
through soil once enflamed
TT Raw sprigs spike mead, sprouted from the red
seed of Rowan
TTT Cities grew above water on Alder, with whittled
weapons and flutes that sing
TTTT Slumping but never rending, life without end does
Willow foresee
TTTTT Sacred Ash stood that the physical world might
uphold the sky

⊥ Hawthorn paints dual faces of thorn and charm that
balance herein
⊥⊥ Wherever the house of summer opens, its powerful
Oak door is the noble way
⊥⊥⊥ Then must acquiesce to the dress of Holly, the gown
of snowflake theatre
⊥⊥⊥⊥ Blossoms of Hazel explore feminine forms that curl
in cuneiform beauty
⊥⊥⊥⊥⊥ And fertility bursts into the burgeoning
dowry of Apple

╱ From Vines flow succulent wines through passion's
veins of egos frothing
╱╱ Ivy revives the verdant life and life-indestructible

╫ Reeds fill with song of wind-voices from pure lungs of seraphs

╫ Brace! Strife-twisted blackthorn has a wife of autumn yellow-bloom

╫ Honor the Elder of white petal musk to inhale youth and hope

╼ We learn to stand as true as the Fir, pillars that mark the forest within

╼╼ Gorse seeks Light despite a course of night where the higher road begins

╼╼╼ Heather is elixir, intoxicating love-woven meadows from heaven

╼╼╼╼ Victory will fiery Aspens, young or old, whisper in wisdom-visions

╼╼╼╼╼ Gnarled like a Yew, thy inner ancient church is wisdom-known

The **Ogham alphabet** is the ancient Celtic alphabet, preceding the overrunning Latin language of the early medieval period. It consists of a mere twenty alphabetic symbols in which each letter/symbol represented a sacred tree to the Celts. Each tree also had sacred meanings assigned to it.[10] This is an example of a spirituality tied to deep-rooted connection to the natural world.

____

10   *The Ogham Alphabet Explained*, Ogham.co, https:// ogham.co/ogham-alphabet/, 2020.

The Seat of Dalriada

When one arrives, the glen appears
Its story now, no glory steers
The reins of fate preside here now
no Guinevere, no cricketeers
just grazing sheep beside the cow

Columba claimed the Scottish heart
Encircled cross would he impart
before the crown where truth would fail
before the horse's harnessed start
that plowed the field and river vale

In stone a footprint crowned a lad
who'd own this throne on River Add
who'd threaten kingdoms with a sword
if only for the crest and plaid
where clans would strive with strained accord

I climbed your rock to read your rune
and gripped its cliffs like bald baboon
Where love had leapt your dew-slick sides
where we have traipsed and men were strewn
and dripped deep red where grass resides

You filled my flask that Celts prescribe
with mead that mystic saints imbibe

I drink to your forgotten race
through hearts that spanned from tribe to tribe
and strove the age-long steeplechase

Dalriada (Dál Riata or Dál Riada) was a Scot-Gaelic kingdom that stretched across the western seaboard of Scotland to the north-eastern corner of Ireland, and north of the Antonine Wall built by the Romans from west to east across Scotland. The Romans called the Irish Celts of Antrim "The Scotti" who originated in Ireland. Dalriada reached its height in the 6th and 7th centuries in what is now Argyll (Coast of the Gaels) in Scotland and part of County Antrim in Northern Ireland. After a period of expansion, the kingdom eventually became associated with the Scot-Gaelic kingdom of Alba. St. Columba played no small part at its zenith of power.[11]

11　Marsden, John, *Sea-Road of the Saints*, Edinburgh, Floris Books, 1995.

Angels of Kilmartin Glen

The cairns like giant hooves afield
resound the depths of death again
But roses climb here unconcealed
with angels of Kilmartin Glen

The trees here echo raven's caw
where sun is lion, sky is den
And billows spill their gray guffaw
with angels of Kilmartin Glen

I stare to prize the river's glint
in raindrop-light one cannot pen
The sparks of Spirit striking flint
with angels of Kilmartin Glen

We witness drifting, walking rain
We know not how, nor why, nor when
'The Hidden' riffs profound refrain
with angels of Kilmartin Glen

This day spent in the wondrous **Kilmartin Glen** was an excursion in the rain. We hopped from one sacred site to the next with good raingear and finally sat down to lunch in a glass walled garden restaurant that allowed the view of the valley from our tables. The rain picked up intensity as we were served, and I and a few of my comrades could not help noticing that the rain was coming down in shafts, that appeared to be walking, windblown across the field of view like angels with 30-foot legs. This continued until we were done eating. It is quite difficult to speak when in awe. I found myself swallowing tears because it resonated in me deeply that this was the holiness of the natural world. Its vivid animation (and imagination!) was beyond the logical, finite mind of our physically limited reality.

May Day

Jubilant day filled an urn of sky
polishing ice-gutted alleys of granite
Elders invoked gods and visions
that seasons measured in moons
might peach with holy trees
That speech disappeared on the
vines of wisdom from heaven's mystery
tendrils round all created things

Children of the world whirled into dance
From their nexus of hand and heart
grew zest purified in mirth
The fruit of festive rite

A wreathe for a warrior-king
feted the summer song
That fire might stay Winter's
hollow, brittle wand
That a burning torch
might keep the tribe and hope alive
To be nurtured in a cave
as seed of the same Father-Sun

until The Radiance returned

Veil of Love

You, O Hebridean twilight, hung your soft vista
Where I couldn't reach, so you merged with me
To transport my heart, harmony-swung
To its bonds of belonging to beauty inside

You, O chaste beloved, to welcome summer rain
Floated words of mist like silvered sheathes
Across the heather groves that camouflage me and
Saturated my tribute of fasting at this outpost of dune

You, O teacher of dreams, abscond with my slumber
With voice that calls, finger that directs, and wisdom
That reminds disquieting shrines of ivory and ebony
Only holiness unites black and white in the heart

For You, O heavy veil over vast eternities, lies my soul
That longs, my anima that aches, my or Your will
That breaks the anchors of thought and taut reflex to
Plunge the River Love, sweeping my little all to You

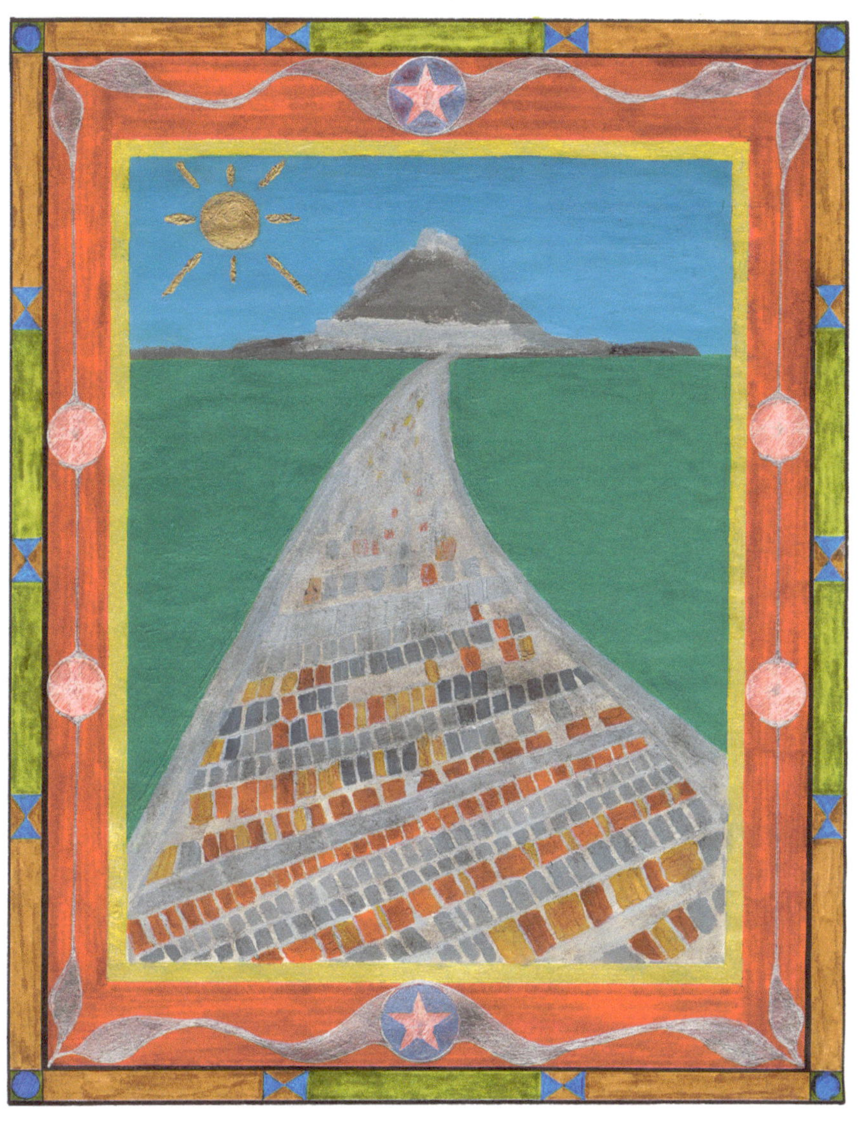

SAINT MICHAEL'S MOUNT, CORNWALL

Saint Michael of the Tides

When sailors saw the flames of God ignite the skies
Horizon to horizon pealed an ocean blue
That purified the beauty it would dramatize
For there was every threat of death a sailor knew
For theirs was hope, so tightly held to crystallize

The British Sea for fishermen was all they knew
And Celts arrayed two mounts with bastions
stacking high
The whitecaps thrashed these giants who would chaw
their spew
But Michael throws a beacon that will never die
But Michael seeks the ships that rock and sea
would strew

With all my Celtic spirit I would fight and vie
To harvest from the sea to fill the village store
And Michael stayed the hand that beckoned
Death to buy
My little life that flagged upon its threshing floor
My whittled cross became my shield of Michael nigh

The great archangel staves the cask of Life to pour
Before the little lives can thrash the rocks and rave
Protector of the land and sea, not troubadour

Bright Michael is and was a son of God to brave
The holocaust, the lost, befallen every shore

Mont-Saint-Michel (Brittany) and Saint Michael's Mount (Cornwall) are located on opposite sides of the English Channel. Two dramatic sanctuary-castles originally built to tower over the coastlines, they were both dedicated to **Saint Michael** the holy Archangel in the 8th and 11th centuries. They both belonged to the Benedictine religious order at one time. Both were inspired by visions of Saint Michael, who was reported to have appeared numerous times throughout western Europe in the early and middle medieval period. For the newly Christianized Celtic peoples, Saint Michael was the defender of land and tide. Each sanctuary became a pilgrimage destination for the church.[12]

12   *Mont-Saint-Michel, Saint Michael's Mount,* The Editors of Encyclopedia Britannica, Accessed May 15, 2019.

Celts, Saints, and Mystics

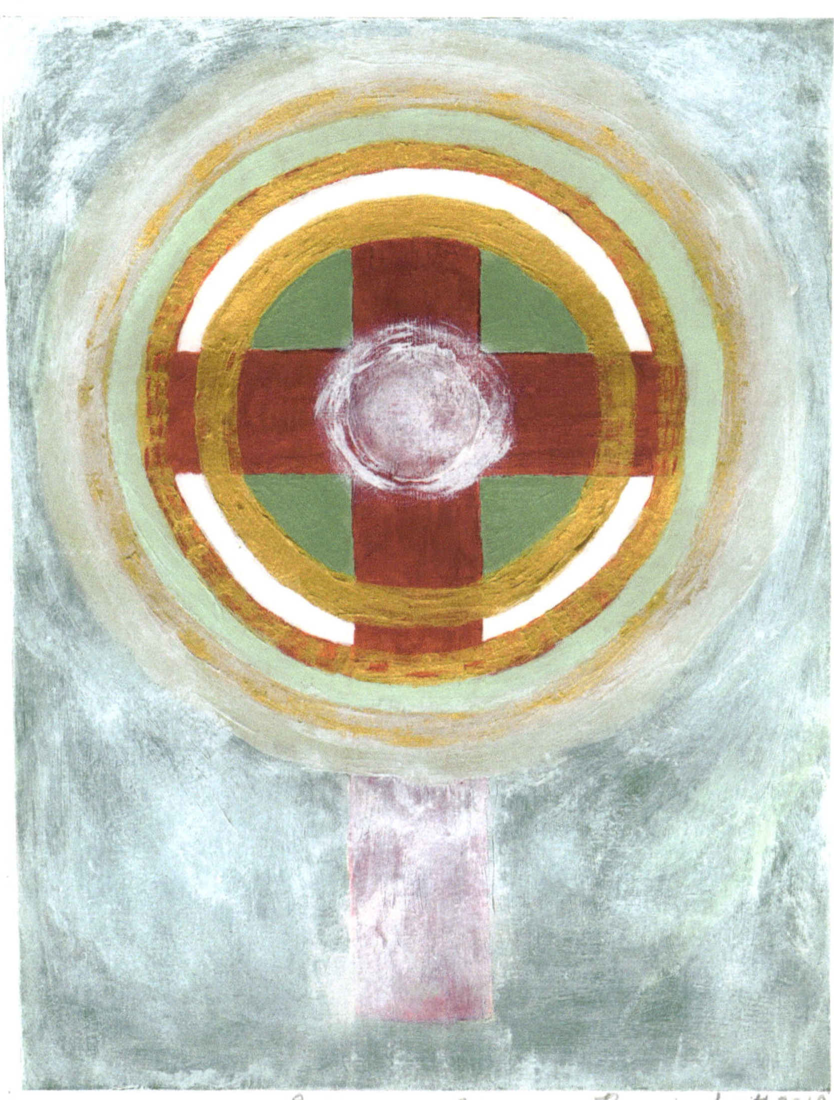

PATH OF THE CROSS THROUGH THE
CLOUD OF UNKNOWING

This symbolizes the journey of the soul, nurtured by the birth of the Christ in the heart. Through contemplation in the Cloud of Unknowing, an awareness ever expanding in God follows the path of the cross via the three gold rings of infinite Trinity.

The Monastic

I contemplated mantric shores
and living mist upon the moors
when breath of heather blushed the lea
medieval chants by ancient sea
would reeve galactic jewels that kite
the indigo of endless night

Would I transcend the walls of home
to gust the vast and stellar foam
of countless swirl through dizzy urn
to dusty shell of self return
transformed in tranquil hall of stone
with zeal I held for God alone

I once dreamed vividly that I was watching a monk, myself, hard at work in a candlelit scriptorium in a monastery somewhere in Scotland. I was illuminating the page of a hand-copied bible. It was the 15th century. The name given me was Uriah. I looked out from the monastery doors across the heather and peered up into the amazing starlit sky. The last thing told me in the dream was that I was in Kirk. Not knowing what that word meant, I looked it up in my parents World Book encyclopedias dated 1965, and on the map there was a place designated as "Kirk" on the western shore of Scotland. Kirk is the word for "church" in Scottish.

Monasticism was the hallmark of early Celtic Christianity (latter 4th C. to 10th C.). This was a time when Rome's establishment as a religious center of power was secondary to the Byzantine rule from Constantinople. Due to the dismantling of the Roman Empire, Rome's influence was all but removed from northern mainland Europe and the isle of Britain (410 A.D.) because of the pullback of Roman forces from these regions. The ensuing armed conflicts vying to fill the power vacuum destroyed many structures of an abandoned society. What we know today as Ireland, Wales, Isle of Man, Scotland and other Celtic enclaves were left to freely pursue monasticism. Christianity flourished in a decentralized fashion.

Saint Ninnian (c. 432 A.D.)

You had straddled two worlds as the Hadrian
Wall slid away
It was pelted by Celts in the waves of the raids
from the north
For the terrible clouds rose and fell with the storm
of the steel
Much the same as our heels fleeing hills in that cart-
rutted Time

Within you was an octave divine that would
resonate more
With the waves of the seekers, the newborn who opened
their ears
Was your motion of prayer overlaying the
children of God
Whom demented in mud likely called in futility's Time

For I searched your white church for its light under
armor-less coats
And found three and white terns wheeling every
direction through air
For that sphere above land that sustains us is earthward
and skyward
Then inward and outward, then backward and forward
through Time

I was Gael, I was Pict, I was Briton on roads after you
For the Romans brought you to be balm for the kings
of this land
And with hands of great love you came slaying and left
us as slain
But your love can't elude us by mile nor erase us by Time

Saint Ninnian (Ninia), a Briton-Celt by origin, is one of the most venerated saints of Scotland. He is commemorated as "Apostle of the Southern Picts." Our great authority, the Venerable Bede, mentions St. Ninnian in his Ecclesiastical History of the English People (731). Ninnian was a friend of St. Martin of Tours and fashioned his whitewashed/lime church in Whithorn, the *Candida Casa*, after that of St. Martin. Whithorn became famous as a monastic center, and St. Ninnian's miracles continued even after his death. Whithorn was a place of great pilgrimage in the Middle Ages.[13]

13   Lapa, Dmitry, Orthodox Christianity, *Saint Ninnian of Whithorn*, https://orthochristian.com/73449.html.

Sedulius the Poet (c. 5th Century)

In the court was a poet, right hand of the king
Who in victory raised more than voice to take wing
From his satchel and buckle that shined in the light
Came the vellum and verse he composed with a zing!
That his lord held the lead to flout bravery's might
To record the bold deed and shout bravery's might

When Sedulius left his own Scotia to flee
To his love for the learned, the world would soon see
But before he was priest or a priest's acolyte
Wore he reds and some yellows, refined with esprit
For this bard was like Bede but his saffron was bright
It was starred on the sleeve in no fashion too bright

Now when he was a lion to all of his foes
And their arrows within him ignited his throes
He befriended a man who was skilled, The Cartwright
Who would build him a cart for wherever he goes
Like a steed over gravel and roads of dark night
To thus travel, unravel the code of dark night

Then he turned to the lady to juxtapose fate
By her light in the gloom it was never too late
At her table of happiness, no appetite
as he pondered no thing that a man could conflate

For his verse had a need for this spiritual sight
Privy purse he received from this spiritual sight

So Sedulius wrote for the lady in Rome
He created her antiphon, verses, and tome
It was clear that the poet, a gentile with plight
Laid career at the pulse of the church's great dome
And was called to this mission at Rome's ornate height
And installed for tradition his poem of great height

Sedulius was an Irish Celt from the Scotia region (present day northeast Ireland/Argyll, Scotland). He studied under Archbishop Ailbhe (Germanized to Hildebert), one of the four pre-Patrician saints in Ireland. He traveled to Athens, founded a school of poetry, and taught philosophy in Italy. Best remembered by his composition "Carmen Paschale," since published in every century. From it, the Entrance Antiphon for the Feast of the Solemnity of Mary, Mother of God, January 1, as well as in the Saturday Mass of the Blessed Virgin Mary: "Hail Holy Mother! Who gave birth to the king who rules Heaven and Earth forever."[14]

Bede; Saint Bede the Venerable, (735 A.D.), Early doctor and scholar (monk) of the Church who is considered the Father of English History.[15]

---

14 D'Arcy, Mary, *The Saints of Ireland*, St. Paul, Irish American Cultural Institute, 1974.

15 Wikipedia Contributors, *Bede*, Wikipedia, The Free Encyclopedia, Accessed October 4, 2019, https://en.wikipedia.org/wiki/Bede.

Saint Tydfil of Wales (480 A.D.)

Like a still loch in the depth of dense forest

A point in an age of darkness reflected the light
The light that sires the one life in this lower world

And thus, between portals of birth and death
she exposed The Mercy

> She, by the winds that race with Mercy
> was flute for the spirit of life
>
> She, by the streams that ripple Mercy
> was subtle silver that gleams
>
> She, by the thunder unfurling Mercy
> was chalice full of rain
>
> She, by the sun's magnificent Mercy
> was vista parading dawn
>
> She, by the sea that churns with Mercy
> was vat for the stew of Creation
>
> She, by the trees that bend in Mercy
> was shelter for innocent ones
>
> She, by the Earth that blossoms Mercy
> was holy basket of plenty

And she, by her union of Faith with Death
why Mercy emerged from eternity

Saint Tydfil was a martyr killed by pagans. She led a holy life in the country of the Taff River valley in Wales, sparsely populated by Celt farmers and their families. She became known for her compassion and healing skills as she nursed both sick human and animal. She established an early Celtic monastic community, leading a small band of men and women. Her home included a hospice, out-buildings, and a scriptorium. There she lived quietly, bringing hope and support to the people of the Taff valley.[16]

16 Orthodox Outlet for Dogmatic Enquiries (OODE), Biographies, Saint Tydfil, Martyr of Wales (†480). http://www.oodegr.com/english/biographies/arxaioi/Tydfil_wales.htm, 2005, (Source). http://onepearle.blogspot.com/2009/08/st-tydfil-martyr-died-c480-ad.html.

Saint Illtyd the Knight (c. 480 A.D.)

A royal Briton ate the fruit that Knowledge blessed
Before the grief of life was taught through plague
and drought
He spoke beneath the apple bough of wisdom's nest
Of eloquence and arrogance of battle's clout

For sometimes strength must humbly die a self-
honed wretch
A sacrifice of knights who fight a fatal bout
Initial peaks in life are not the final sketch
The journey draws what everlasting truth will out

For angels fare to bring a voice from heaven's breast
Conversion seems to pierce the skin of hearts too stout
Saint Illtyd hid these secrets under soldier's vest
That resurrection's slashing charge was soon to rout

As when he tamed a stag and served the king his catch
That he who serves reserves a harvest God will tout
As angels slay the demons gleaned to humbly fetch
The wayward who must nobly slaughter every doubt

For Illtyd's second life was filled with deeds that best
The fame of knighthood where he only carved a notch
To joust this gauntlet's avenue is lifelong test
That draws the nod of Seven Holy Flames Who watch

Saint Illtyd was a knight and cousin to King Arthur. He spent much time in Brittany and is revered there (and Wales). On a military mission, he had a deep conversion experience and later became a priest in Wales. He was known for wisdom and had a number of disciples whom he led to the priesthood. Miracles were ascribed to him during and after his life on Earth.[17]

---

17 Baring-Gould, S., and Fisher, John, *The Lives of the British Saints ... and Such Irish Saints as have Dedications in Britain*, Vol. II, London, Charles J. Clark, 1908.

Saint Keyne the Virgin (505 A.D.)

At times her skin had shone like sun or snow
Majestic clouds can turn my soul to rain
That dove and angel swill on hill below
Among her oak and willow, elm and ash
Where lion yawns and lies upon its mane

Believe me when I stoke such things aglow!
For wonders cannot cease from saintly strain
As dove and angel glide the winds that blow
Among her oak and willow, elm and ash
And tender love for tenant, lord, and thane

Her healing spring, like arrow from a bow
Spouts waters even giants can't contain
As dove and angel slake from sacred flow
Among her oak and willow, elm and ash
Her shade beneath the bugles of the crane

If love defines the wine of Christ's Bordeaux
It grooms the human vineyard for champagne
For dove and angel daffodil will grow
Among her oak and willow, elm and ash
Her crown outshining those of Charlemagne

Saint Keyne, (also referred to as Keane, Kayane, Keyna, Cenau, Cenedion, Ceinwen) was a holy woman who traveled widely through what is now Anglesey, Wales, and Cornwall. She is known for a famous well in Cornwall and has dedications to her throughout the region.[18]

18   Horstmann, C., *The Lives of Women Saints of our Contrie of England &C.*, London, N. Trubner and Co., 1886.

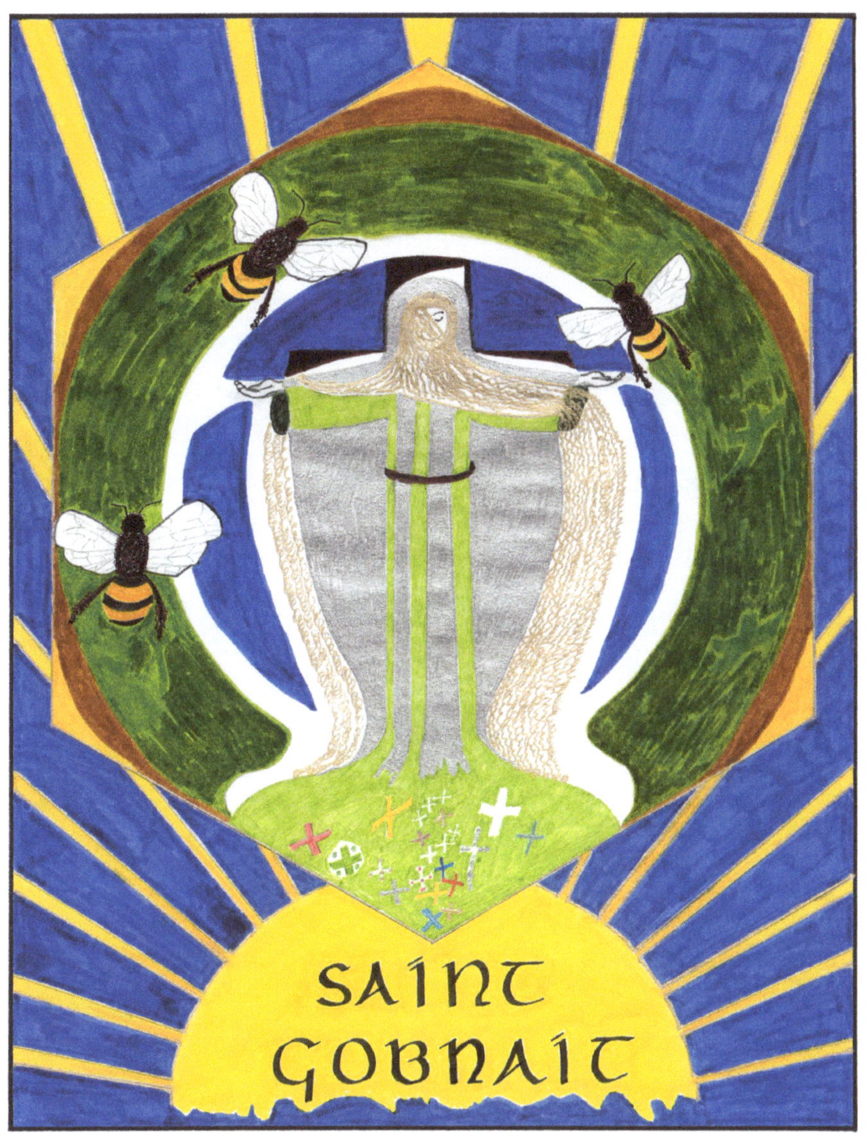

SAINT GOBNAIT OF BALLYVOURNEY

Encompassed in the divine architecture of a honeycomb cell, Saint Gobnait created her own hive to be the vessel to bring God's love and light into the world. One with the earth and sky, and the creation between. The three bees are symbolic of the Holy Three of the Christian Godhead.

Saint Gobnait of Ballyvourney
(c. 6th Century)

You lifted your eyes from the hills of Aran isle
from a door of a chapel of your devotions
You must've seen what I saw, The Uncountable
in the flitting sparks that incite this fabled sea

Though we're numbered, no human is measurable
nor even the warm glint of God in the insignificant
As in eyes of the lame, of those who only rise once
like the little waves that wage to purge this shore

And how often we shepherd despair's bad luck
It looks like a flock atop an icy outcrop that
skids our valleys of elsewhere. So we latch onto
pyramids or drink from the rivers of no return

To attain resurrection, pilgrims seek fields of
luminous deer, harmony of bees, and ten million
watts of wild lightning to purify, weld, and reclaim
what will frame the power that won't disappear

Mother Abbess, sweet children remember to hive
the legends that story your race, where we hover
to see by your light, a glimmer that waxes realms
of our squalor when we clearly glimpse you

Saint Gobnait (gob-net) was born in County Clare, Ireland. In order to escape a family feud, Saint Gobnait fled to the Aran Islands. There she built a church, which is still named after her, but angels told her that she would find the place of her resurrection where nine white deer grazed. In southern Ireland she founded the church of Kilgobnet (near Ballyvourney), and her convent, where she saw the nine white deer.[19]

19 O'Hanlon, Rev. John, *Lives of the Irish Saints*, Dublin, James Duffy and Sons, 1875.

Saint Moninne of Killeavy (517 A.D.)

When I gave a vow by the breath of my God
His prophet veiled me by the Holiest Three
My lace made a cross that I laid on a rock
that sprung into brooks through the willows and me
and sung with the sparrows through willows and me

When I was a sheep in a puddle of God
I stared into all the reflections of me
Not one was my image, divine is my flock
that eats golden wheat of the Holiest Three
that bleats at the gate of the Holiest Three

When I found a church on the mountain of God
Whose summit surmounted the All I could see
Surrendering love to the many who knock
were virgins to pillar my palace to be
to burgeon with silence my palace to be

When I am abundantly empty with God
and everywhere witness the Holiest Three
My soul can swim out of its shell in the lough
and swell with a current from river to sea
Through shell of my soul flows a river to sea

Saint Moninne (mon-ni-na) was an Irish abbess of Killeavy, who is said to have been veiled by Saint Patrick himself.[20]

---

20 O'Hanlon, Rev. John, *Lives of the Irish Saints*, Dublin, James Duffy and Sons, 1875.

Saint Buite (521 A.D.)

You pumped bright trumpets and strode for the Lord!
And wore a clean sackcloth sewed with a cord

You slumped like sunset and won its gold crown!
The Milky Way's epic glowed like a sword!

You stumped the cynics—God calls us to shine
Your torch for souls indeed slowed the dark horde!

You bumped into clouds as prophet renown
And colored Columba's road when you roared!

You dumped my heart in your coffers divine
And strode with the Picts, and healed where
they warred

You clumped love's words in your boat. They
won't drown!
As love sent you west to row a long fjord

I trumped great feasts and found ennobled wine
Faith was the guest who swallowed the whole gourd!

I jumped your great seas and splashed, never bored!
Thumping full moons to gong ode to the Lord!

Saint Buite (boot-ye) descended from the Chieftains of Munster and founded the monastery at Monasterboice, home of the Cross of Muiredach, one of the finest examples of a Celtic cross in Ireland. He performed many miracles of healing in his life. He was well traveled through Italy and Germany and prophesied the birth of Saint Columba (Colm Cille).[21]

---

21 *Omnium Sanctorum Hiberniae,* http://omniumsanctorumhiberniae.blogspot.com maintained by Marcella, an Irishwoman 2012-2015.

Saint Brigit, the Mary of Erin (524 A.D.)

The shrine of this island
was forest until torched by The Inextinguishable
A flame thrown from standing stones
festive as an ancient dancing yew

Your tale of the Gael
would groom furrows in lands where no Roman fell
Your province by necklace of earth,
wind, fire, and water

Where the press of your footsteps
was beaten flat by armies of Time who savor sadness
yet recall your image shimmering
the lough and salmon-fat river

Forget us not in your secret prayer
when we wait by the well under sky's sprinkled blessing
whose voice buries the stillness
that claims the soul in every Eire that was

Because bubbles on a stream
like prayer, ramble flat through stony beds
until their flow imitates beauty itself
popping without stopping

Like complexion unblemished
when the mind rinses the matter of many vanities

to let the holy speak unfettered
through all speechless planes

As a door in Kildare
illumined Sanctity Herself, which will not bar
nor ever jar the lantern you carried
now eternally borne

Saint Brigit of Kildare (one of the three Patron saints of Ireland along with Saint Patrick and Saint Columba), is the most famous female leader of the early Celtic church. She governed both women and men in her double monastery at Kildare. Nuns at her monastery are said to have kept an eternal flame burning there, a custom that may have originated with female druids residing at that spot long before the saint arrived. Even though the holy fires have long been extinguished, the reputation of Brigit as a spiritual guide remains.[22]

22   Sellner, Edward, *The Wisdom of the Celtic Saints*, Notre Dame, Ave Maria Press, 1993.

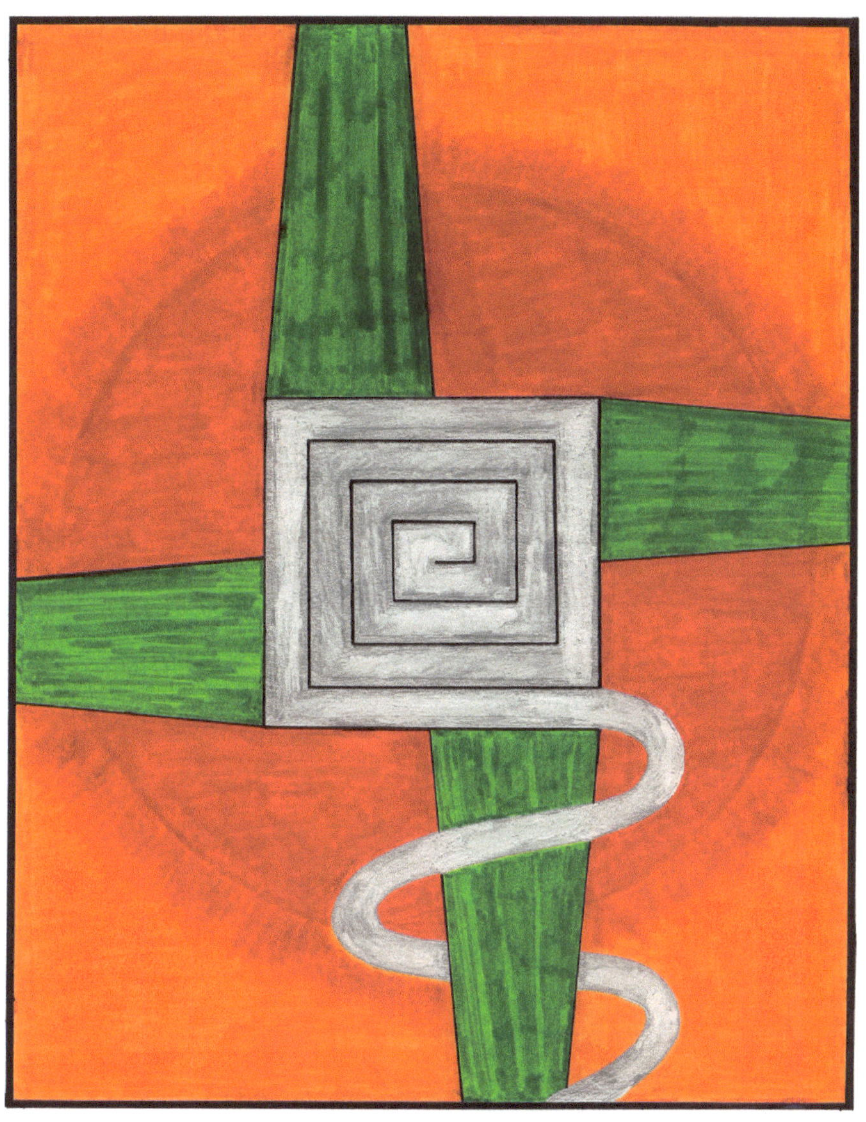

CROSS OF SAINT BRIGIT

Meditating on the symbol of the famous Brigit's Cross, the divine impulse of good at its infinite origin winds outward to heal the world. Similar symbology is Moses' serpent on the staff in the desert, which pointed to Jesus on the cross and the mystery of redemption. The background of fire portrays spiritual fire, the fire of the soul with the embalming Holy

Spirit, dominating the crucial turning points in life, as if one is touched by fire. Saint Brigit is said to have tendered an eternal flame at her monastery.

Saint Brigit of the Vale (524 A.D.)

In the land of the Picts where she freed many souls
Was the Mary of Erin determined to go
And quite stout were the folk under yoke of life's tolls
Like the highlands that stand before evil and woe

Was the Mary of Erin determined to go
With a band of her virgins to sow a great field?
Like the highlands that stand before evil and woe
They had planted a cross behind Michael's white shield

With a band of her of virgins to sow a great field
On the coast, on the mountain, in valley they prayed
And had planted a cross behind Michael's white shield
Where the lost can find Christ in the world's
masquerade

On the coast, on the mountain, in valley they prayed
When the soul shines as bright as the moon on a pond
Where the lost can find Christ in the world's
masquerade
Why the Mary of Erin used love as her wand

Where the soul shines as bright as the moon on a pond
It's humility's muscle that opens The Way
Why the Mary of Erin used love as her wand
To move obstacles blocking the light of each day

It's humility's muscle that opens The Way
And quite stout were the folk under yoke of life's tolls
To move obstacles blocking the light of each day
In the land of the Picts where she freed many souls

The Irish always had a most tender love for the Blessed Virgin, and **Saint Brigit** was called by the Irish saints "the second Mary," "the Mary of Erin" (and "the Mary of the Gael"). Nothing could give us a more exalted idea of her sanctity; nothing could express their love more forcibly. To place her near the mother of God would be a great honor; to place her next to her is the greatest mark of respect they could pay her. Mary was their refuge in every danger, and to honor both by the same act, they called them by the same name.[23]

23 *The Life of Saint Bridget, The Mary of Erin* by an Irish Priest, New York, 1861.

Saint Enda of Aran (c. 535 A.D.)

There is one fleeting love that brings love to its knees
One eternal worth living through storms from without
On an island the stones were for Enda the keys
With a breeze that breaks backs, even warriors devout
In the silvery mist they grew gray on The Way
In the foam that slays shore with a stiffening clout

In that time of the monks they were gripped by a vow
And their sacrifice offered a victim divine
For the spawns of the world were its slaves up to now
And the journey within, it was far from benign
Through the silvery mist that might rainbow The Way
In the light that abounds from the One in the Trine

To be guided by light would firm Enda insist
To peer out like a patriarch over the sea
As one fights through the gnats and the gulls with a fist
Like the slaughter of meaningless things that could be
Through the silvery mist that was paving The Way
Wherefore Enda the cloud of unknowing sought he

Without mead, without meat, without ale or green dell
Came a voice that sang true from the vine of the heart
And it drew from the waters that garden that cell
Because Enda would render his soul's divine art

Through the silvery mist that he braved on The Way
For what rises from Earth tugs the heavens apart

Saint Enda, the patriarch of Irish monasticism, is described as a famous ex-warrior who abandoned the world in mature life. He was promised to marry a nun who was in the convent run by his sister. The young nun died suddenly and Enda, through deep remorse and reevaluation of his battle-ridden life, converted to Christ and eventually was given the Aran Islands to create his mission on earth on Inis Mor. His monastic order was quite austere even for those times. He was revered by many of his saints and those on the mainland who came to be known as Ireland's most profound of the golden age of Celtic Christianity in the isles.

"The Way" was an early Christian term for the path of Christ. The victim divine was seen as Jesus offering Himself as a victim. Many disciples as monks sought to imitate that virtue of sacrifice.[24]

---

24 D'Arcy, Mary, *The Saints of Ireland*, St. Paul, Irish American Cultural Institute, 1974.

Saint Non of Wales (c. 540 A.D.)

With barley bread and melted snow, to God I
pled a boon
Withholding want, I drained its swamp and let it
fade to dune

A hidden ark of prayer will dare to voyage to redeem
Withal, these waters spread with grace as swans
parade lagoon

My gift of Life conceived a son to teach the highest truth
For threats to end my pregnancy, my bosom
flayed typhoon

My monastery housed the Life that gathers
deer to stream
Within that Life I nurtured hearts that love had
weighed and hewn

On hills of wilderness I grazed, like bees, with
sweetened tooth
Withstanding wind and sleet I reaped the pollen
they'd festoon

My burdened soul delighted to unearth this
lifelong dream
Without a word I thanked the angels for my
spade and spoon

Each soul must build a blaze to light the world from
sacred booth
Withhold not Life, withhold not love, nor
barricade the moon

Non, or Nonna, the mother of Saint David of Wales, was one of many Celtic missionaries who travelled from Ireland and Wales through Cornwall and on to continental Europe. In an eleventh century hagiography we find that despite the pious words used to describe David's birth...his mother, who may have been a nun, was raped...Both mother and son, however, went on to become the two best-known and loved saints of Wales. Her tomb survives at Finistere, Brittany.[25]

25 Sellner, Edward, *The Wisdom of the Celtic Saints*,
Notre Dame, Ave Maria Press, 1993.

Saint Ciaran the Younger (549 A.D.)

If I could have died at thirty and three
and left you inheritance valued by me
You'd need divine light for fortune I found
not coin of the realm that's buried aground

If I could have died at thirty and three
and left you a harp abandoned by me
Let strings be the strands that roam through your mind
melodious nights I hope you will find

If I could have died at thirty and three
and left you the bullion hoarded by me
You'd peer at the priceless brightness that slings
a toroid of suns in cymbals and rings

If I could have died at thirty and three
and left you an empire Ciaran gave me
I'd leave you an isle, the tomb of each wave
whose countless we count and sow not a grave

Ciaran (keer-en) of Clonmacnoise, the Younger, Abbot (also known as Kieran, Kyran, Ceran, Queran). Born in Connacht, Ireland. Saint Ciaran is one of The Twelve Apostles of Ireland. A student of St Enda on Inishmore, Aran Island, he was given the vision of the school he was to build. He built the famous school at Clonmacnoise Monastery and lived only seven months after its completion at the age of thirty three (33). It's generally agreed that the Twelve Apostles of Ireland came from this monastery.[26]

26 O'Hanlon, Rev. John, *Lives of the Irish Saints*, Dublin, James Duffy and Sons, 1875.

Saint Modomnoc (c. 550 A.D.)

If by touching a wave, I should change
then likely the wave also changes
If by staring at stars of vast range
this world through my eye rearranges

When the world followed me as I sang
I sang 'til alone and kept singing
Until waters from rock with life sprang
like startling flocks that bolt winging

And as I had to sail across sea
to pollenate Christ on each shore
What I brought besides honey and bee
would cause them to hunger no more

A student and disciple of St. David of Wales, **Modomnoc** eventually returned to County Kilkenny, Ireland, bringing with him the skill of raising hive bees. He is known to have brought the bees from Wales to Ireland. Most of his life is known to us through the life of Saint David.[27]

---

27 *Omnium Sanctorum Hiberniae,* http://omniumsanctorumhiberniae.blogspot.com maintained by Marcella, an Irishwoman, 2012-2015.

Saint Ita (570 A.D.)

In the meadows of faith, in a convent for home
It was Ita the holy, who groomed with a comb
all the flaxen-faced youth in the novice's strife
for Killeedy was hearth to her spiritual life
and Killeedy made art of her spiritual life

More than mother to Brendan and saints in her care
she would gather their milk from the stall of her prayer
By the sunrise she fixed exact moments of days
for their hearts to awaken to God and to praise
for no hearts are forsaken in God's divine rays

Yet the simplest present, the warmth that she shared
was from solitude, fasting, a love undeclared
From this field of her strength grew a faith undeterred
in miraculous ways that would flower the Word
in oracular days where the insects had whirred

For the clan had adopted a prophetess true
whose religion was virtue, although it was new
And her well was a vehicle healing the ill
that would carry the poor to the King on the Hill
and would marry the poor to the King on the Hill

If true faith in the heart is my beggarly bowl
shall I sip from her buttercup deep in my soul

For this truth can't be traded for lucre's gold chain
for the tender of love is a cross, should we deign
for the tender of love is not loss, but a gain

Ita (also Ite or Ide) is, after Brigit, the most famous of Irish women soul friends. Her hagiographer even describes her as a second Brigit. A sixth-century abbess, Ita founded a monastery in County Limerick at Killeedy (which means Cell or Church of Ita). She came from the highly respected clan of the Deisi, and her father, like Brigit's, was resistant to her becoming a nun. After gaining his permission, Ita left home and settled at the foot of Sliabh Luachra, where other women from neighboring clans soon joined her. There she founded a monastic school for the education of small boys, one of whom was (Saint) Brendan of Clonfert. She evidently had many students, for she is called the Foster-mother of the Saints of Erin.[28]

28   Sellner, Edward, *The Wisdom of the Celtic Saints*, Ave Maria Press, Notre Dame, 1993.

Song to Saint Brendan the Navigator
(577 A.D.)

Upon the sea you peered from lofty cliff
In cowhide boats you'd search for storied lands
where whitecaps' spray and seadog's nest collide
where crew believed that monsters slunk the depths
Though God was all, but not at all was sudden
to strengthen backs of saints to rudder life

And we are who must take the task of life
to thrive on rocky coast to scale its cliff
Dispatched to climb a wall that stalls is sudden
with staff of hope to conquer snowcapped lands
And crossing where crevasses gape their depths
the very instant love and faith collide

No doubt, no doubt our angels will collide
like oars that stroke a wave invading life
For those who fly and sail the crest and depths
might soar like hawks to claim exalted cliff
And hawks, who own no breeze, no clouds, nor lands
yet sack their prey whose freakish call is sudden

In times of test we bail when squalls are sudden
When lightning parts, then nimbus skies collide
with inner soil that once was savage lands
We'll navigate with stars that guide a life

We'll glide a wind to veer away from cliff
We'll call the Nameless from our very depths

True living is the music of the depths
If first we walk then run, a fall is sudden
but earns the taxing stride of narrow cliff
And climbing with this effort won't collide
with what projects a soul to higher life
our inner summit far above these lands

And at the southern pole my spirit lands
where glaciers ever blue to snowy depths
compound the winds that twist a human life
Where brutes of rock would form, atolls are sudden
as ice makes isles of sky when rocks collide
And where our planet tilts its frigid cliff

And once we dare the cliff of Brendan's lands
we pilgrims dream, colliding steeper depths
as voyage-life made Brendan's landfall sudden

Saint Brendan was an Irish priest who established his first monastery at Ardfert near present-day Tralee, then Clonfert in 561 A.D. He was a renowned and regular voyager of the North Atlantic. Ergo the appellation, St. Brendan the Navigator. Established in the kingdom of Dalriada a monastery some years before, Columba established his famous monastery on Iona, no later than 574 A.D. Brendan, though 20 years senior to Columba, was in his inner circle. He accompanied him to both Pictland to meet with King Brude, King of the Picts and to Hinba (Jura) for the power conference with the priests Comgall, Cormac, Cainnech and headed up by St Columba. It was Brendan who witnessed a ball of spiritual fire above St. Columba's head. The tales of Saint Brendan's voyages were a medieval classic, taught at the universities/ monastic schools well into the Renaissance.[29]

---

29 Marsden, John, *Sea-Road of the Saints*, Edinburgh, Floris Books, 1995.

The Steed of Saint Michael the Archangel

It was Michael the Bright, on white Brian rode he
For no lightning has ever out quickened this beast
As Saint Michael on Brian could flash to Capri
Not as desert monastics that strode the Mideast
But by will of the wind that can rollick the sea
Just as fast as white horses that come to save me

In the Hebrides, Brian's quick wings you can see
Like a bride to God's breath, like a high flight of geese
Was there ever a steed of such great pedigree?
And he races with freedom, a race that won't cease
Like the will of the wind that can rollick the sea
Alike all the white horses that come to save me

From the mount of each day I shall call the Culdee
Who, asleep in my heart, was not ever deceased
There's One Love and One Life that our fears
at once flee
Where we find the true wedding and find its true priest
With the will of the wind that can rollick the sea
That unleashes white horses that come to save me

With the Belt of Orion and Mystery's key
On a saddle of clouds made of ivory fleece

Our Bright Michael appears, astride Brian will be
At a precipice rearing for headlong release
With the will of the wind that can rollick the sea
And with all the white horses that come to save me

On the isle of South Uist, Outer Hebrides, I traveled to its southern tip where there is a strait separating it from the island of Eriskay. Across the causeway I found a church on the point of Eriskay opposite South Uist. The church was named after the great Archangel **(Saint) Michael**. I ate my lunch there beneath the sky of rippling clouds racing the wind. I paid respect and prayed at the statue of St Michael at the gate of the church. From there I wound my way down the hill to the rest of the island to be discovered. As I turned toward the end of the road at the ferry point, I was stopped in my tracks by a herd of white horses who had wandered up onto the road. I admired them in awe. How beautiful they were with their long white manes and graceful white tails. It was a truly inspiring sight of beauty. One horse even came right up to my window. They were of course immoveable from their "post position" on the road, and I had no dire urgency to move them in my marvel. When I returned to my hotel that evening, I recognized for the first time, not one, but two framed portraits of white horses on the wall outside my room. The only ones in the hotel. They were telling me so blatantly, how little I had to do with the planning of this journey.

So, I do not recount this story because it supports a legend of Brian, the white steed of the great prince Michael. But I tell it because it supports the true reality. This event was an outer physical manifestation. I must attest also to its incorruptible inner reality.

A Culdee was a monk attached to a monastery. The Culdee reform movement in the 800s, led by Saint Maelruain, mentor of Saint Aengus, was a more austere form of service by essentially working with the hands to support the monastic group and living a life in the monastery devotionally.

Brian was the name of Saint Michael's steed, famed for its swiftness and its whiteness.[30]

---

30 Carmichael, Alexander, Carmina Gadelica, *Hymns and Incantations*, Edinburgh, Floris Books, 2006.

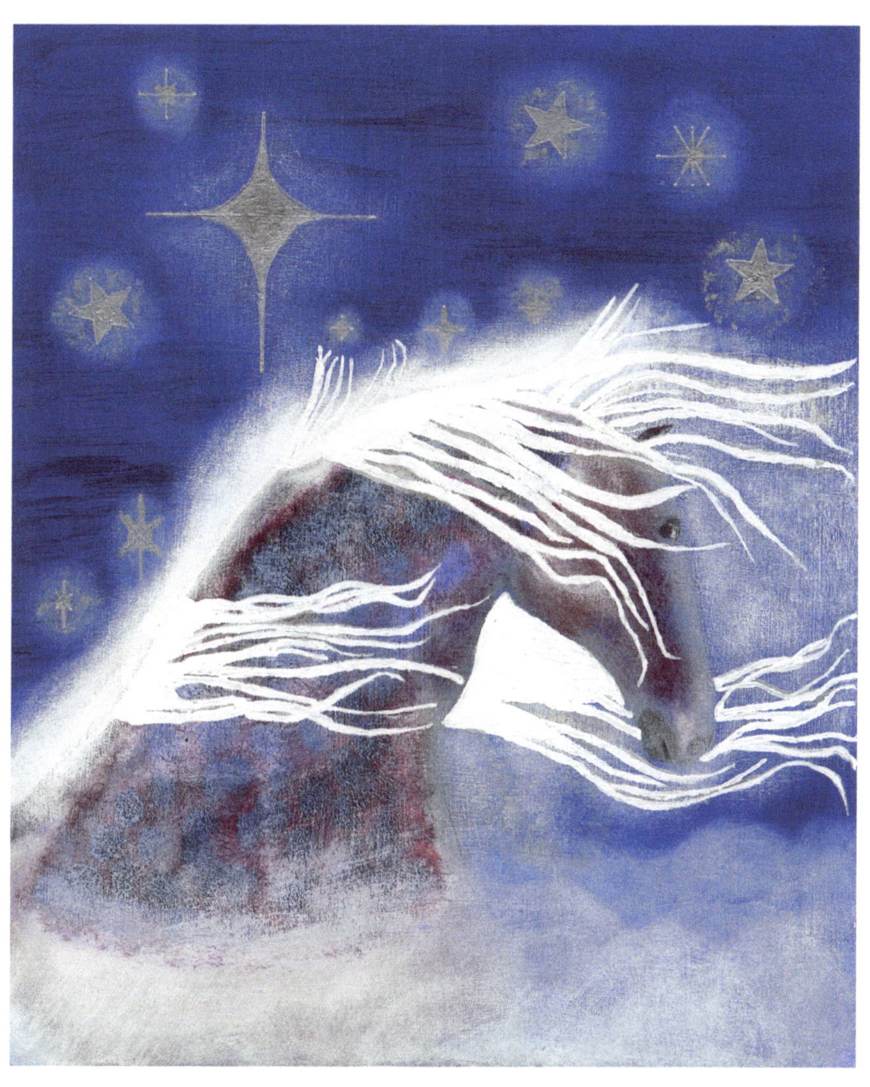

BRIAN, STEED OF SAINT MICHAEL THE ARCHANGEL

White Martyrdom of the
Island Messengers

As the nautilus gyres, I ponder ethereal shell
Where the waves come a-spiraling, foaming the spray
they expel
Through the surface poke seals, the unsinkable lives of
the finned
While the rocks with the lichen-mosaics are bleached as
if skinned
As the dunes on this shore lay out loneliness where I
could dwell

Here I found the white martyrs whose fathers arose
from Carmel
But these deserts were roads through an ocean and
pathless through hell
I pretended I left all my tribe just to follow the wind
As the nautilus gyres

Then I knew I must open my heart to the sky
and its spell
For these clouds, like the seagulls, will ride the
perceptible swell
Could the love that created these innocents ever
have sinned?
Or is love in all hearts, beneath sun and the sea,

underpinned?

For pure wonder resuscitates worlds from this

deepening well

As the nautilus gyres

Essentially, **white martyrdom** for the Celtic monk/religious was the sacrifice of everything they held dear for the sake of the Christian gospel. In that society, one's loved ones and family were the dearest, and thus a life of giving up that comfort for the missionary journey was the ultimate sacrifice, short of death.[31]

31 Marsden, John, *Sea-Road of the Saints*, Edinburgh, Floris Books, 1995.

Song of the Red Martyrs

One hundred stars would tumble from the sky
When angel cries resounded planes of bliss
For those above the human world would sigh
When Wisdom's timber fell by fire and this:
The sweetness of a psalm and antiphon
That greeted slaying raiders with its kiss

For on the shores of Scotia, Eire, and Farne
Grew sanctuaries for the song of Christ
That soaked in breeze where foreign boats would warn
Of sails that Norse announced about their heist
But sweetness from the psalm that's sung at dawn
Is greatest in the voice that sacrificed

The chosen few whom seers knew to tell
Would speed the holy relics into flight
And if they turned to watch the smoke of hell
Or hear the wailing of the wretched blight
Deep sweetness of their psalm was found upon
No quarter given in the depths of night

The tales of noble women, men, and brave
Elect a triumph we find hard to see
Because the axe of battle and its knave
In blood rewrote the ancient history

The sweetness of the psalm that lingers on
Relieves us of their loss and butchery

And now the tyrants of this world have slain
Our guiltless Mother Nature every day
Upon Her cross the kingdoms shall remain
And from Her bounty all of life purvey
For sweetness from a psalm will launch a swan
Who then can fly where evil cannot prey

The definition of **red martyrs**, in this early medieval period approximately 380 A.D. through the Viking Age (793-1066) and beyond describes those Celtic Christians who gave their lives for the cause of Christianity. They witnessed, sometimes by merely confessing their faith, or being in the way of an invading army, and were executed at the hands of non-Christian groups.

Saint David of Wales (589 A.D.)

A white dove lit upon your shoulder
for the same reason it came to me
to coo in the ear of the earthbound
about the nimbus of the pure, to air the
gifts of the mother cedar, whose deep
breast feeds a forest with her heartbeat
moistening wild leeks with divine dowry

So we, to a path through ethereal fields
Our strength is not mettle fashioned from ore
for contemplation's fruit is death and dying
Though we stagger like Atlas, lugging the
world to this weightless grave of awareness, our
fate will fall into an air of The Fathomlessness
into all there is and all there ever was

And this plummet unburdens the spirit
wending a sanctified way through a seminary
of simplicity, clear wind blowing through the
mind, acoustic heart resonating through words
solitary prayer pouring its many textures
so that all our deeds spill from the fount of
devotion, translucent rivulets running to God

Saint David was born ca. 500 A.D. and studied under Saint Paulinus to become a priest. He founded 12 monasteries from Croyland to Pembrokeshire. He travelled to Brittany (modern day France), another Celtic community, and added to the church in building a foundation there. A number of his churches were built in south Wales after his return to Wales. David was known for the extreme asceticism of his monastery, which was based on that of the Middle Eastern desert fathers and mothers.[32]

32 Baring-Gould, S., and Fisher, John, *The Lives of the British Saints ... and Such Irish Saints as have Dedications in Britain*, Vol. II, London, Charles J. Clark, 1908.

Saint Moluag of Lismore (592 A.D.)

This Celtic elf from holy mountains gathered Picts
and kingdoms
A road he'd taken through the world for crucifix
and kingdoms

His chapel rooved with solitude, the sod of sons of God
On Lismore stood his sentry to the River Styx
and kingdoms

His times of action woke the clans and those
who'd often nod
By ode he vowed to serve the kings with pyx to fix
the kingdoms

He sailed the northern sea that led to Orkney's
isles abroad
He leapt from ladders that descend to politics
and kingdoms

On currach he had sailed to seas of ice that clogged
and thawed
His abbey grew a vine that twined the lattice-sticks
and kingdoms

The martyrdom of saints was at the hands of
who maraud

For who destroys, destroys the same sad lunatics
and kingdoms

His urgent storms that sought the North, we get, and
wholly laud
Refulgent was his holy rage with relics, wicks,
and kingdoms

Saint Moluag (muh-LOO-uh) was one of the original twelve priests, whom Columba took to Dal Riada, the Scotic-Gael kingdom on the western coast of Britain, and thence to visit the Pictish King Bruidhe to establish détente for the monastery on Iona, located in the borderlands of the Picts. Saint Moluag made several northern voyages to the Orkneys and beyond in search of the farthest North Atlantic isles for the white martyrdom. Attributed to him are healing wells, important central Christian churches in pagan Scotland, and miracles.[33]

33 O'Hanlon, Rev. John, *Lives of the Irish Saints*, Dublin, James Duffy and Sons, 1875.

Saint Columba (597 A.D.)

Unlike the Sun Who grants a golden platter
For all the goals in life we've ever schemed
The clouds that gray our thoughts erect no ladder
To mesa that expands a life redeemed
Yet sun and moon will rise as light cascades
As Beauty, Love, The Good have always dreamed

You sail to islands seeking waters pure
You take provisions God beside you lent
And buffet waves that make the way obscure
The One Who Always Was will give assent
To souls who start these dauntless escapades
That Beauty, Love, The Good won't circumvent

With battle axe you had to smash through matter
Another day would haze ascend from sea
And in that vagrancy with shield a-tatter
The Beauty, Love, The Good and your Marie
Led you, of God, to conquer these crusades
Now warrior of the blessed fleurs-de-lis

Columba, Colum Cille, through winds that tore
The sail of life that changed your waterways
You claimed as Christian druid you'd restore
The Beauty, Love, the Good whose proteges

Expanded like the heather that invades
Each moor and holy island in your bays

Availing words of love would set your ladder
You built it for the tribes who just survived
Upon this mountain saint would strive with satyr
Where poverty prevailed, injustice thrived
But Beauty, Love, the Good fed your brigades
Whose citadel, Iona, had revived

Saint Columba's name (Colum Cille) in Irish means "Dove of the Church." Columba is a Patron Saint of Ireland along with Saint Brigit and Saint Patrick. Born in Donegal of royal blood, he established the famous Iona monastery, ca. 565 A.D. He had many visions and accurate prophecies which Adamnan confirmed in his biography of Columba. Columba, via Druidic cultural inheritance, assumed that high priest's power relationship with kings. From a warlord heritage, he set his power base in Iona where he established détente with Bruidhe, king of the Picts and the kings of Dalriada and the Ui Niall clan in Ireland.

The fleur-de-lis became a symbol of the Blessed Virgin Mary after the baptism of King Clovis of the Franks, who was said to have received the lily from her.[34]

---

34 Marsden, John, *Sea-Road of the Saints*, Edinburgh, Floris Books, 1995.

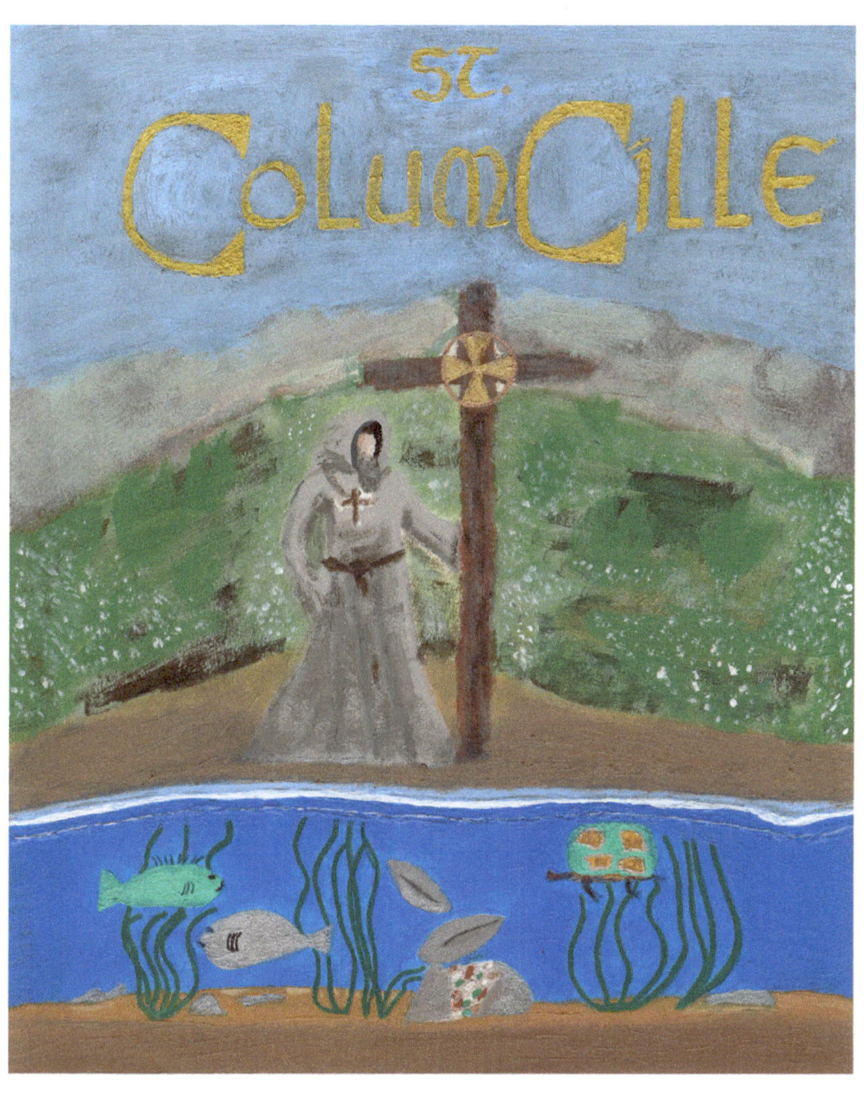

SAINT COLUMBA

Saint Melangell of Wales (607 A.D.)

Tattoo her soul with juniper and oak
Their seeds of love the wind has freed and sown
Look now, before the forest dons its cloak!

In dew and dripping sap my hands will soak
This luxe of nature can't be overblown!
Tattoo her soul with juniper and oak

The throb of night the bulging frogs will croak
And hares that come to snuggle, softly moan
Look now, before the forest dons its cloak!

Her inner fire plumed eternal smoke
Each secret sunken glade to her was known
Tattoo her soul with juniper and oak

The innocents that lark about awoke
The nightingale in thicket on its throne
Look now, before the forest dons its cloak!

The angels from the woodland often spoke
Ten thousand sentinels no one could own
Tattoo her soul with juniper and oak
Look now! before the forest dons its cloak

Saint Melangell (mel-en-geth), to live a religious life and escape political marriage, fled from her father's dominions and secreted herself among the hills of Pennant, Wales (called after her Pennant Melangell), in Montgomeryshire, within the principality of Powys. There "she lived for fifteen years without seeing the face of man, serving God and the spotless Virgin." After witnessing her holiness in defending a little wild hare, her new landowner, Brochwel, gave her lands "for the service of God, to be a perpetual asylum, refuge, and defense, in the honor of thy name." She gathered nuns around her and became the abbess of her convent.[35]

---

35 Baring-Gould, S., and Fisher, John, *The Lives of the British Saints... and Such Irish Saints as have Dedications in Britain*, Vol. III, London, The Honourable Society of Cymmrodorion, 1911.

Saint Mungo/Kentigern (614 A.D.)

They shed adrift your mother to the sea
to sever from her soul her other half
Embracing that savannah's cold debris
she strode its darkest canyon with no staff
a canyon marked for fatal epitaph

For here, her vigil gave that passage life
And here, the pure, assured before the Thrones
The Great Alone would bless abandoned wife
and baptize saint and son whose fate atones
all those who follow God through great unknowns

For you, our dear one, lived the loving Word
a river cleansing all within your path
St. Kentigern, you'd learn to lead the herd
if straight by that, a bloodless martyr's bath
a bath that grants a savior's aftermath

A fast of forty days distills desire
and waxes virtue's nights of sultry sweats
Yet sang his soul in wastelands with a lyre
and sat before a sun that never sets
like steel that hones a soul and surely whets

For Glasgow bore its own Melchizedek
his gift revealed before the crown and queen

He wore compassion's yoke around the neck
of which the saints saw such a crown serene
a crown that only saints have ever seen

The renowned apostle of Strathclyde and present-day Glasgow was raised by St Serf after a miraculous rescue from the sea when his pregnant mother was cast adrift. **St Mungo**'s dedications are numerous throughout England, Scotland, and Wales. He taught in both Wales and Scotland, and produced at least four miracles, the symbols of which the city crest of Glasgow depicts.[36]

36 *Omnium Sanctorum Hiberniae*, http://omniumsancto-rumhiberniae.blogspot.com maintained by Marcella, an Irishwoman, 2012-2015.

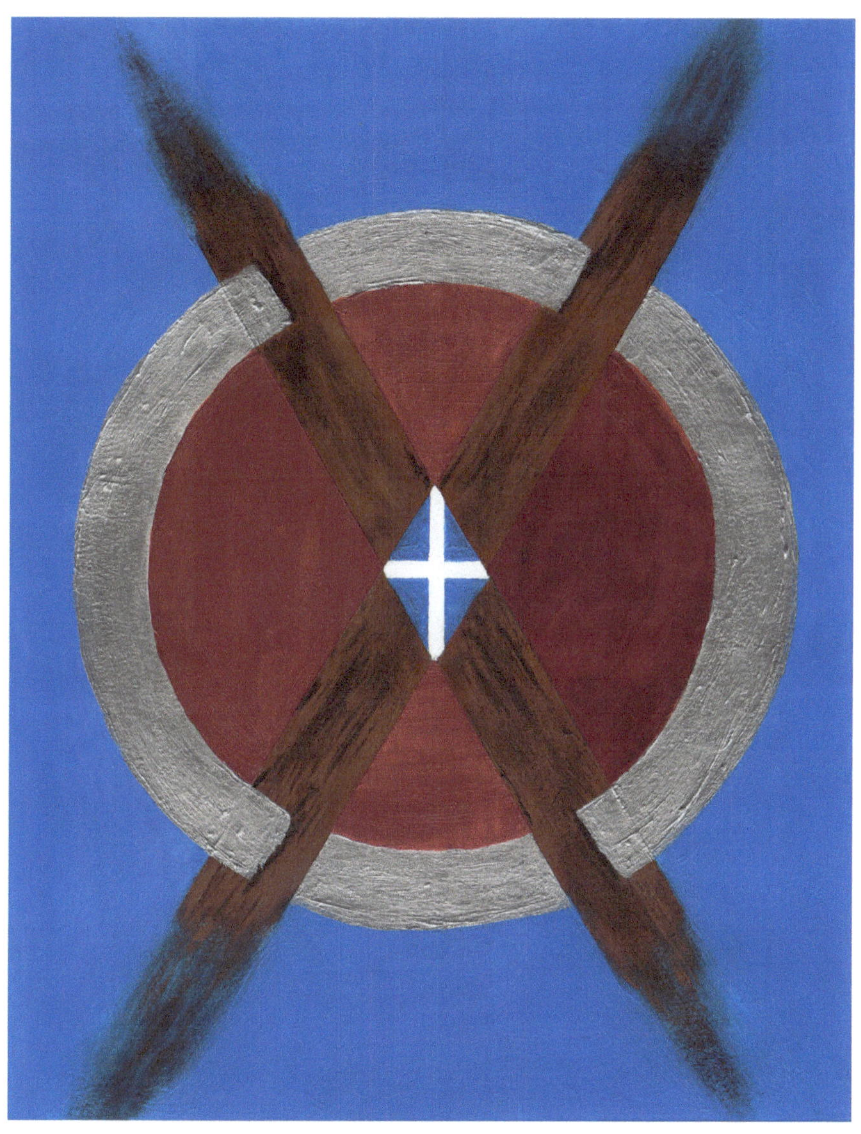

SHIELD OF SAINT ANDREW

Saint Andrew became the patron of Scotland after his relics were brought to the island in the Middle Ages. Devotion and pilgrimages followed. It was commonly believed that the Apostle Andrew had chosen the Scottish people to care for and honor his relics. The Saltire flag's colors at the center of the wooden Saint Andrew's cross reflect the deep relationship with Scotland and Saint Andrew. The worldly trials that produce sacrifice (red) of the ego rests inside the silver ring of God's omnipresence. God envelops and cares for all humanity, and in this case, the Celts, Jutes, and Anglo-Saxons who became the Scottish peoples.

Saint Columban (614 A.D.)

He was threshing our souls in the fields of the king
And by bending to water that wells from a spring
In the cup of his hands there could be a chateau
Or a cold falling stream that could change every thing
Through his hands in a blessing from God it would flow

When I walked across Gaul with no minstrel that sings
With the psalm of the wind and the cosmos its strings
With the words of that kingdom that never let go
We shall find the true heart, even though it has swings
From the crescent white moon to the life here below

In the threshing of souls I found fields for the king
Who has sent me to draw from the wells of his spring
And I dry-stacked a wall to protect the chateau
Of the good who stood small in this cosmos of things
As the leaves change the trees in the seasons that flow

For I walked across Gaul, and that century sings
By the harp of a Gael that gave melody wings
With the words of a kingdom that legions let go
I pronounced from the heart in a song from the strings
That blend fire and wind with the rain and the snow

Columban, also known as Columbanus, was perhaps the greatest and most influential of the Gaelic missionaries to work abroad in continental Europe. (Author's note: At that time, Europe's Christian infrastructure was severely fractured by constant wars after the withdrawal of the Roman legions.) This then, was the Irish monk reckoned by Pope Pius XI "among those distinguished and exceptional men whom Divine Providence is wont to raise up in the most difficult periods of human history to restore causes almost lost." To him goes the credit of raising up a legion of saints, of recruiting and setting on the march the most considerable force in saving the faith in Europe. His monasteries, most notably Bobbio in Lombardy, produced illuminated medieval literature classics too numerous to mention. Columban's immediate followers have been credited with establishing 100 monasteries.[37]

37　D'Arcy, Mary, *The Saints of Ireland*, St. Paul, Irish American Cultural Institute, 1974.

Saint Kevin of Glendalough (618 A.D.)

Between the loughs you dredged the truth, and truth, a
flawless sieve
You grabbed a flag of lightning knowing what it
was to live
You floated on the wedding song of water and the wind
and carried sanctity that blows to any life chagrined

Between the loughs that splash the mind there is a
sunlit dome
You left your footprints on a land, once strolled by
noisy gnome
A castle for a different kind, the humble and the meek
find higher states that ever wait to draw those
called to seek

Between the loughs there is a tide that washes
as it crawls
erasing him, who hopes to be The Watcher on the walls
Behind the rising fog of fear is not what any deemed
but mirrors this eternity in every day God dreamed

Between the loughs, The Life is one and cycles on
through time
with subtle blend of cosmic strings connecting
every clime

For angels populate the places we can never see
As long as ogres slay the Earth, apart we'll ever be

Your spyglass to Divinity, like geese that fly the glen
would see Creation's constant glow from eagle to a wren
Between the loughs, Saint Patrick saw a prophet
on a throne
a barefoot prince in cattle skins who slept no night alone

Saint Kevin (Coemgen), at the age of twelve, was given by his parents to three holy elders for his education and care in the monastery. Eventually he was ordained a priest and established his chief monastery at the valley of two loughs (lakes), Glendalough. A seer, a mystic, and miracle worker. A peer of Saint Columba's time.[38]

38 O'Hanlon, Rev. John, *Lives of the Irish Saints*, Dublin, James Duffy and Sons, 1875.

The Holy Isle of Saint Laserian (639 A.D.)

Of the flames that will climb up the vine that will
flourish from youth
It's the flame of the heart that is pruning the cane
for rebirth
It was Pilate who asked, "What is truth?", at the
trial of Truth
Finding sanctum in One Who could radiate love
from the heart
That all flesh might refresh by The Light that had
fallen to earth

On Laserian's island his cave was a seashell and plain
He was pilgrim to Rome and he left with the
vestment of priest
To return to an isle of a wilderness hard to explain
Finding sanctum in silence Laserian loved
from the heart
Where The Hidden illumines the void like the sun
in the East

When alone might an angel appear after visiting hell
There's a voice that articulates insight for
visions supreme
From the one who comes calling the soul to rely
and retell

Finding sanctum inside let Laserian love from the heart
As our nest, but a cloud, holds a test and a silvery seam

It was Aaron who girded The Law with the
parchment of zeal
As angelic tornadoes stood tall for the wandering clans
There was Miriam dancing with love they could see and
could feel
Finding sanctum in them would Laserian love
from the heart
When imagining tambourines jingling awhirl
in the sands

Of the myriad spirits the army of God can amass
With the chant of the righteous and just in the
glorious din
Any saint, perhaps we, can arise and aright the morass
Finding sanctum Laserian found in true love
from the heart
from an island that summons a soul like a sweet violin

Saint Laserian, colloquially called Molaise (muh-los'-ye), was born in Ireland and was raised and schooled at Iona as the fosterling of Saint Murin. He travelled to Rome and was ordained a priest by Pope Saint Gregory the Great. Returning to Ireland, he made hermitage at times on Holy Island, off the east coast of Arran Island in the Inner Hebrides. He became abbot of the monastery at Leighlin, Ireland.[39]

39 O'Hanlon, Rev. John, *Lives of the Irish Saints*, Dublin, James Duffy and Sons, 1875.

Sonnet to Saint Eanswythe of Folkestone (640 A.D.)

Her childlike heart was pure as light from heaven
An angel's stairway climbs that sky of joy
A milk-white lamb caressed this coast to Devon
Rejuvenating love that found this boy

I know a nun, my quiet sun. No doubt
She sent a psalm of rain to bathe my land
Estranged by love, to sea I then set out
And sonneted her shore of soaking sand

My heart was flung, a skipping stone times seven
In all directions, love I saw—but Oy!
Then water turned to wine and faith to leaven
The bread of life that no one can destroy

Through tresses blonde her visions I shall comb
The sacred locks of God that call me home

Saint Eanswythe (pronounced inz-with), also Eanswida, Eanswith(a), Eanswide, Eanswyth; the daughter to King Edbald, and Queen Emme, who reigned in Kent, niece to Edburge the saint. She renounced the world from her infancy, bearing in her heart the purpose of religious life and perpetual virginity to serve the Lord. The father, being convinced with reason and wise discourse of his daughter, yielded to her request and built her a church and monastery in honor of St. Peter, in a place called present day Folke-stone, nearer the sea and remote from the concourse and trouble of men. Thought to be the first monastery/convent in Britain. Died at the age of 24. Devon(shire) and Kent are southern coastal counties of England.[40]

---

40 *The Lives of Women Saints of our Contrie of England &C.*, C. Horstmann, London, N. Trubner and Co., 1886.

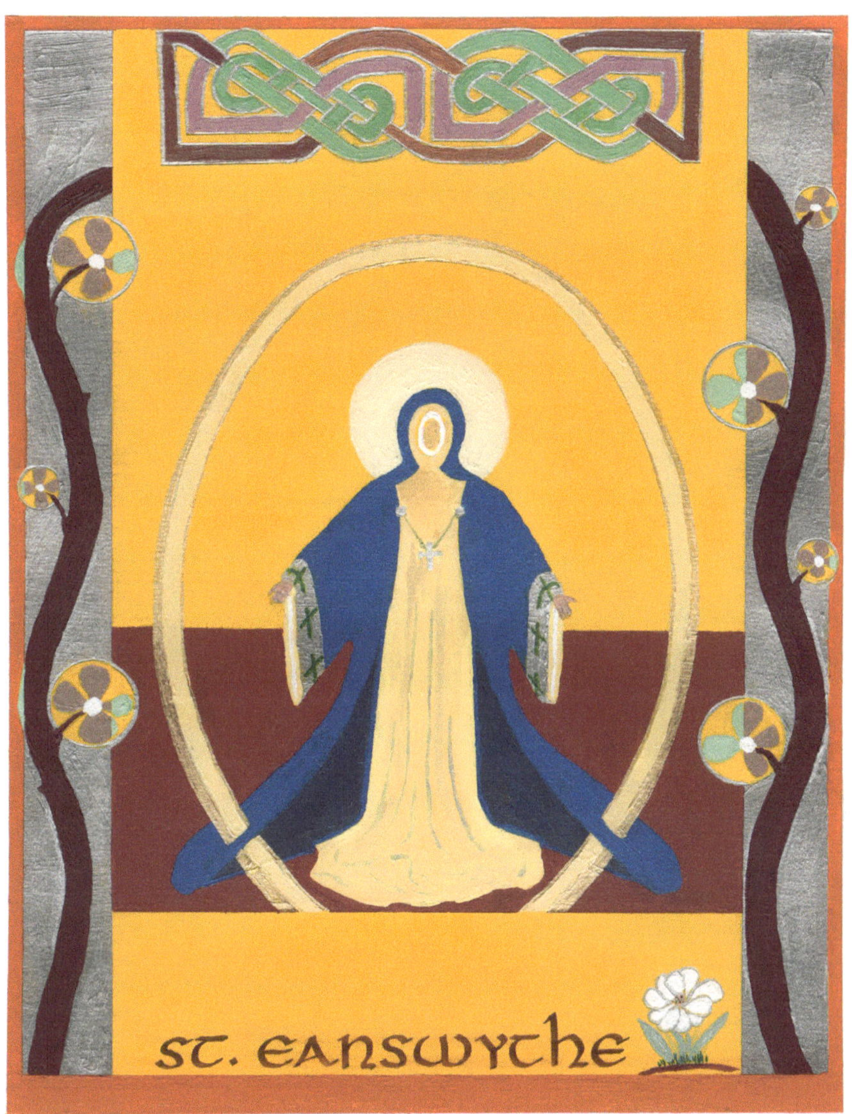

SAINT EANSWYTHE OF FOLKESTONE

Saint Eanswythe was known for miracles before and after her death. Christian faith grew as a result, which is depicted by the bordering vines (Christ) and flowering offshoots. Saint Eanswythe's devotion to Blessed Mother Mary is indicated by the White Campion flower, native to Folkestone, Kent, in the bottom right.

The Well of Saint Winifred of Wales
(650 A.D.)

Eleven virgins entered where
she stoked a hearth of reddened coal
And filled the bowls both round and square
so rife with each disciple's role

Each strife to tame by living words
The Life that plumes the rarest birds

The river from her mystic well
of Spirit to the Celts would speak
with healing, vice the ruse of spell
with voice that mansions Christ's mystique

With poise to build a faith that girds
With noise that raises firebirds

The hoax of death has shackled souls
who grieve and totter hope to hope
But there above the crags and holes
from cliff The Shepherd guards the slope

Forever drifting precious herds
He ever lifts from thunderbirds

Where frigid currents fill the air
and white-tailed eagles thrash, if cruel

The Holy Three employ with flair
The Undeterred of endless fuel

One energy derived in thirds
The liturgy of hummingbirds

Saint Winifred was known for her sacred well called Holywell. For many centuries of pilgrimage, there was a continuous record of cures and other favors claimed at the well through the prayers of St Winifred. Winifred lived as a mystic in virginity, poverty, and reclusion. She became abbess of a convent built on her father's land and later, having fled from the Saxons, found refuge in Gwytherin, with St Elwy, the author of her first biography. There Winifred and her companion nuns joined an established community where she is said to have lived "as an acknowledged saint on earth, first in humble obedience to the abbess and, after the latter's death, as abbess herself." Sacred birds throughout history have colored the spiritual lore and legend of cultures and civilizations. The dove is a popular example in the Judeo-Christian religion.[41]

41 Catholicism Pure and Simple, *Saint Winifred of Holywell*, Maryla Chidell, posted November 3, 2010. https://catholicismpure.wordpress.com/2010/11/03/saint-winifred-of-holywell/.

Saint Fursey (650 A.D.)

My heart is mast for ship of peace
and through a spyglass we could zoom
to peer horizons flocking geese
where splattered suns my sight illume

    My monastery's lough of dreams
    acquaints no rival, paints no where
    Submerging in the night's extremes
    the watch we kept of silent prayer

The rainbow poured our mystic tea
untainted ark of vibrant light
beginning where the end will be
to guide disciples in their plight

    And on this sea a shipwreck haunts
    a world that's lost to wisdom gained
    For navigating past our wants
    finds God and love still unconstrained

Fursey was the son of Fintan and Ghelghese and was baptized by St. Brendan, who was Fintan's brother. He was announced and glorified beforehand by miraculous signs. Fursey formed his youth in the great school of Cluain-Ferth, and early manifested his sanctity by mighty miracles. He miraculously healed the gamut of human ailments. He became a master and founded in the Isle of Rathmath (present day Lough Corrib, Ireland), a monastery where many disciples gathered around him, among them his brothers, Ultan and Foillan. He was also known for great angelic visions.[42]

---

42   Barneval, L. Tachet de, *The Saints of Erin, Legendary History of Ireland*, John Shea, Translator, Boston, Patrick Donahoe, 1857.

Saint Aidan of Lindisfarne (651 A.D.)

We approach your holy island across sand that seeps
through seaweed and seashells that house
encrusted creatures
It was here your trust in God unmoored your craft
to the world for beings adrift and drowning souls

Your tranquil fire forged a goblet of flaming wine
to purify libation from every lower world
You'd one day quaff victuals of power, light, and spirit
that the soul repours into the souls of all

There was the peace of low tide in your way
Strength of a thousand gulls in your cry from the
sea of God
It carried your seeds that found soil ashore
where wanderers saw you stacking stone upon stone

From traders of slaves you ransomed priests
You wept in shadows of prophecy simply for the lost
You prayed for a shield from heaven
when the highwaymen stalked your flock

I lie beneath clouds on Lindisfarne, among sea grass
blooms bowing low to the will of wind. They tell
how you knelt until pure spirit caressed this wooden
cross, impaling your heart, outside of time, for us

Saint Aidan was the first bishop and abbot of Lindisfarne. A native of Ireland, he became a monk of Iona, where St Columba (Colum Cille) had established his monastery earlier. When King (Saint) Oswald of Northumbria requested a bishop to convert his pagan subjects, Aidan was consecrated and arrived in Northumbria in 635 with his group. He made his headquarters on Lindisfarne. From there, he evangelized and founded missionary outposts, including a monastery at Melrose. Among his Anglo-Saxon protégés were Hild of Whitby and Saint Cuthbert.[43]

43 Sellner, Edward, *The Wisdom of the Celtic Saints*, Notre Dame, IN Ave Maria Press, 1993.

Saint Triduana (c. 7th Century)

At dawning light, the blameless angels, shy before the
sun, blush
Before the dawning light, blushing at the sight of
Endlessness
As ever after comes, dawning ever becomes

In morning dew, the water angels, tiptoes on the
flora, wash
Before the morning dew, washing in the clouds of
Endlessness
As ever after comes, morning ever becomes

In midday glare, the solar angels, surfing astral
shores, splash
Before the midday glare, splashing in the lochs of
Endlessness
As ever after comes, midday ever becomes

In dusking glow, the humble angels, shields for newly
born, wish
Before the dusking glow, wishing from the well of
Endlessness
As ever after comes, dusking ever becomes

At nocturne hush, the cosmic angels, fireflies to
realms, flash

Before the nocturne hush, flashing in the swarm of
Endlessness
As ever after comes, nocturne ever becomes

Triduana (Triduna, Tredwall, Tradwell, Trallen), devoted herself to God in a solitary life at Rescobie in Angus (now Forfarshire). While dwelling there, a prince of the country having conceived an unlawful passion for her is said to have pursued her with his unwelcome attentions. To rid herself of his importunities, as a legend relates, Triduana bravely plucked out her beautiful eyes, her chief attraction, and sent them to her admirer. Her power became curing diseases of the eyes. Many instances are related of such miracles worked, it is said, procured after her death. St. Triduana died at Restalrig in Lothian, and her tomb became a favorite place of pilgrimage. Before the Reformation, it was the most important of the holy shrines near Edinburgh. Her holy well and shrine were unearthed in 1907 and restored.[44]

In a very mystical way all of the natural activities in the Cosmos are performed, including miracles for the sake of humanity's growth in awareness, by the Angelic Hierarchy. Certain of these Celestial Powers are messengers of the divine will of God. It is stated in the Christian Bible (NABRE version), Psalm 90, "Before the mountains were born, the earth and the world brought forth, from eternity to eternity you are God." God created Eternity, which gave permanence, divine identity, and immortality to the Cosmos. But it is through the agency of Time, which the Cosmos creates, that all spiritual and material evolving things of the Cosmos, become.

---

44 Barrett, Dom Michael, OSB, *A Calendar of Scottish Saints*, Fort Augustus, Abbey Press, 1919.

Saint Fiacre (670 A.D.)

Saint Michael, it's true that I followed your wake
To travel in vehicles, wheel-less and shined
For Mary most holy built prayer with my hands
Then I met a saint serenading the poor

To travel in vehicles, wheel-less and shined
Elijah, dear one, fled the world in a flame
Then I met a saint serenading the poor
A troubadour dancing in fire with both feet

Elijah, dear one, fled the world in a flame
O miracle springs trickle hope we confess
A troubadour dancing in fire with both feet
Is walking through gardens infinity blooms

O miracle springs trickle hope we confess!
My choir of angels left Ireland behind
By walking through gardens infinity blooms
Awaiting the lost in the light that won't die

My choir of angels left Scotland behind
Saint Michael, it's true that I followed your wake
Awaiting the lost in the light that won't die
For Mary most holy built prayer with my hands

St. Fiacre (Fiacrius, Fiaker, Fèvre) was born in the west of Ireland and at an early age devoted himself to the service of God. His hermitage and his holy well, on the banks of the Nore, a few miles south of Kilkenny, still retain his name, and were a favorite resort of pious pilgrims. He closed his days at Brie, near Meaux, France, where many miracles attested his sanctity, whilst his shrine became one of the richest and most famous of all that Catholic land. Probably when pursuing his pilgrimage to France that he dwelt for some time in Scotland and reaped a rich spiritual harvest.

Named after him was the well-known French Fiacre carriage and automobile in the late 19th and early 20th centuries.[45]

---

45 Moran, Right Rev. Patrick F., *Irish Saints in Great Britain*, Dublin, M.H. Gill & Son, 1879.

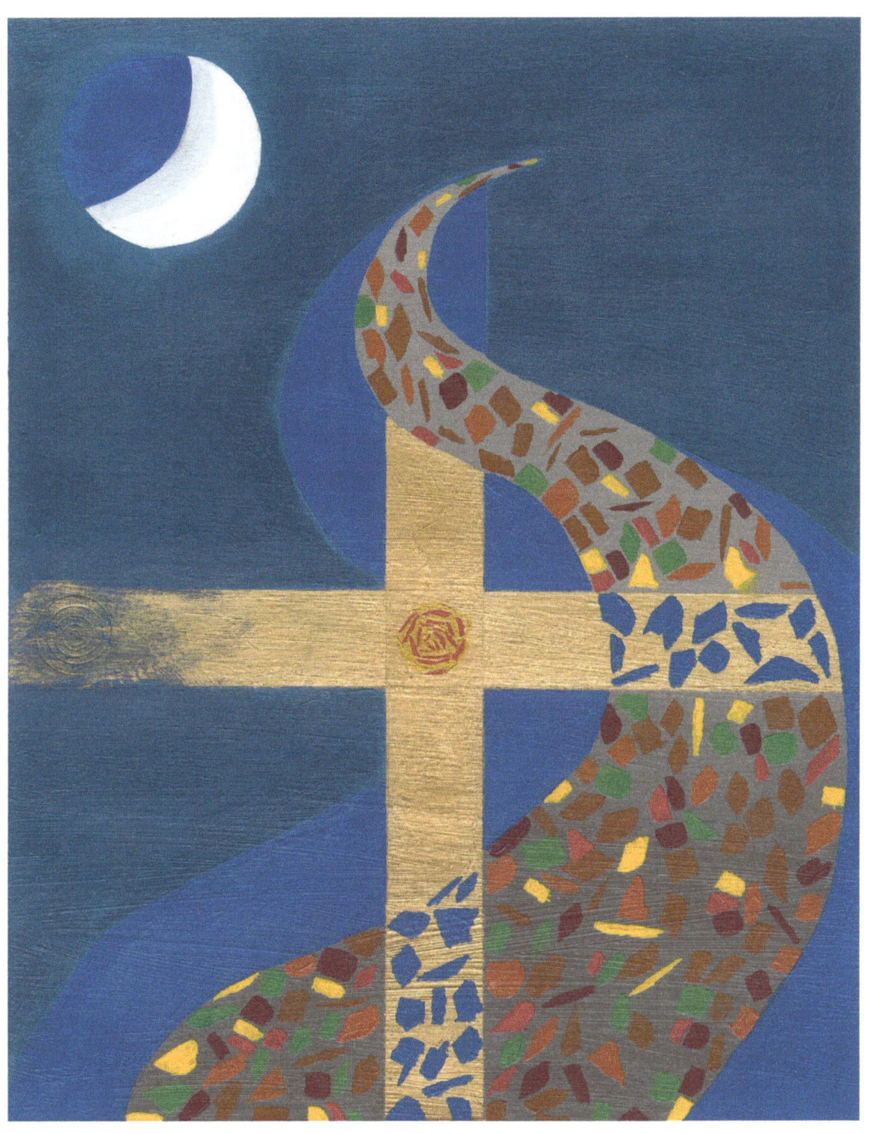

THE MYSTIC LIFE

The rose at the center of the cross is one symbol for the Blessed Mother. For those devoted to Jesus through Mother Mary, this is the sure path. This path takes on a mystical context when the inner revelation of prayer life intersects the outer revelation of conscious life in the world. Therefore, walking both paths is to understand the fullness of God's grace in life.

Saint Hilda of Whitby (680 A.D.)

You were called to the north of the Humber
when Saint Aidan became your new mentor
It was there in recesses by seaside
that your vision and rule became legend

At the headland where stags would come drinking
your monastics were fawns to feed slowly
It was early in winter for Britain
and one sun for one crown had not risen

And unendingly talents spread freely
as you raised for the church astute clergy
for their studies and work became praises
and with flora bloomed north of the Humber

In a childhood of waking to summer
I was called like St. Caedmon to courage
From my heart would I write to determine
why my God woke me up to this labor

In a dream was a woman like Mary
who said, "Blue of the sky is your limit"
She encouraged devotions made holy
by a single point focus on heaven

For it seemed like a dream about Hilda
when her mother revealed the night lightning

of her necklace that shone the world over
to embolden those north of the Humber

Saint Hilda (or Hild) became abbess of Whitby and other monasteries. Saint Aidan mentored her to rule each monastery, and kings and nobles depended on her wisdom. As noted in the last verse, Hilda's mother had a prophetic dream that Hilda's light would reach all of Britain (through a symbolic necklace in the dream that drenched the world with its light).[46]

46 Macdonald, Iain, *Saints of Northumbria*, Edinburgh, Floris Books, 1997.

Saint Bega (681 A.D.)

When she befriended angels, subtle things
Like tender sunlit leaves made trouble fade
For chastity, she cherished more than kings
When she befriended angels, subtle things
Allowed her hopeful faith to grow new wings
Against the winds of hatred, unafraid
When she befriended angels, subtle things
Like tender sunlit leaves made trouble fade

To give to God my freedom, I have prayed
Upon my rosary of wedding rings
My rolling heart afire was one crusade
To give to God my freedom, I have prayed
Since she, the maid, escaped the Viking raid
For miracles of snow and holy springs
To give to God my freedom, I have prayed
Upon my rosary of wedding rings

Saint Bega was known for a number of miracles after she left Ireland's Viking persecution. She escaped eventually to Northumbria where she took up the vows of consecrated religious life.

The Catholic rosary is a sacramental of the church made up of more than fifty short prayers. Designed to be prayed repetitively, the rhythm of a mantra creates for the devotee a singular focus of devotion leading to union with God. Other prayer beads/rosaries of other denominations and creeds have the same mystical purpose. When the Catholic rosary of prayers takes the devotee into the mystical state, each prayer in effect is a wedding ring with the divine.[47]

---

47 O'Hanlon, Rev. John, *Lives of the Irish Saints*, Dublin, James Duffy and Sons, 1875.

Saint Cuthbert (687 A.D.)

There's the spirit of Aidan that called
on the night that his soul was ascending
to the stars like the sea of all souls
if to oracle you for your journey
There's the Celtic hermetical way
a recluse in the arms of The Mother
Who will launch the great flocks through the air
as if winnowing beaches of foam

There's a deep revelation made known
in the luminous pages of Gospel
Where the Ancient and Cosmic pour forth
into floodplains for fishing the Word
There's a treasure you found upon Farne
so much finer and brighter than gold
And the light in the sky of the mind
is invisible light through all life

There's your waterfowl screeching through haze
as they celebrate frenzy with God
For they translate The All through the heart
and where Cuthbert could find himself free

Saint Cuthbert, a shepherd tending flocks at the time, saw a vision of Saint Aidan ascending to heaven the day Aidan died. Cuthbert was to be Abbot and Bishop of Lindisfarne. Cuthbert was an Anglo-Saxon trained at Melrose Monastery, established by Saint Aidan. His sanctity was renown, as were his miracles. He was graced with the gift of healing. His body remained incorrupt for hundreds of years. He often sought his hermitage on Inner Farne, an island within view of Bamburg Castle. The Lindisfarne Gospels, an illuminated book of the 7th C. was dedicated "in honour of God and Saint Cuthbert" by the scribe Eadfrith.[48]

---

48 Macdonald, Iain, *Saints of Northumbria*, Edinburgh, Floris Books, 1997.

Saint Kentigerna (734 A.D.)

Her ancestors' twills wore a shield with a crest
On hills she saw crofters that bled to be blessed
Her journey, unheard of by sage of the clan
A future that Virtue divined in her hand
No mitten for rosaries held in her fist
With song to her Mary a heart can't resist
With song to her Mary a heart can't resist

Some kings and their queens were at war within wars
And courts were not courts, but a den of starved boars
Though 'innocence lost' was the face of an age
The gloves of the holy could save the young sage
To sit in the chapel and never desist
For strong was her prayer to evade to exist
For strong was her prayer to evade to exist

Across the wide sky is a tartan dyed blue
That's wrapped in the joy with the sea and the dew
On continents frozen and beaches serene
On mountains where no one has ever been seen
There, smitten by Michael by holiest tryst
Was longing for faith through the tundra and mist
Was longing for faith through the tundra and mist

And woven through life with the trees that are burled
Her sacraments stirred as the balm of this world

Its light was interior, led not astray
In ocean or desert was not far away
To Britain with Michael on tides that assist
She longed to grow love on the loch of the blissed
She longed to grow love on the loch of the blissed

Saint Kentigerna was of noble Irish birth and dedicated to the Blessed Mother Mary. She fled to Inchcailloch (Nun's Island, named for her) in Loch Lomond, Scotland for political refuge and served as a holy anchoress for the church.[49]

49 Barrett, Dom Michael, *A Calendar of Scottish Saints*, Fort Augustus, The Abbey Press, 1919.

Saint Samthann of Clonbroney (734 A.D.)

In sanctuary of each day she offered up her soul
Her convent opened up its arms, but gold was
not its goal
It made the Age of Eire declare its wisdom for the clans
Besides a herd of half-a-dozen, no one claimed the lands
Besides a herd of half-a-dozen, prayer made busy hands

The turn of clay, or timbers felled, or herding
ridge and field
Or seconds into midnight have a universe to yield
And once aware within that space then once
could be enough
And rest assured its radiance is bright but isn't rough
And rest assured its radiance could vanish in a puff
The strokes of sun and season turned her
contemplation wheel
The King is friend of she who serves with heart's
unbroken zeal
The Trinity, with elegance throughout galactic dome
Will blend the seasons like a ring to race its hippodrome
Where winter, summer, fall, and spring shall
gallop ever home

For Samthann wore her mantle as a mystic
wears the night

Her firmament, the Northern Cross, whose splendor
stars will light
Will cast a compass toward the earth that blinks but
will not fail
She followed clouds of Mercy from the brow
within her veil
She followed clouds of Mercy like a comet's
wondrous tail

Saint Samthann (SOV-hahn) was a noble woman who was married before taking vows. She established a working convent in Clonbroney, Ireland and was known for the highest sanctity, selflessness, immovable faith, and miracles of multiplication and manifestation. She is said to appear in dreams to those in need of her help.[50]

50 Africa, Dorothy, *The Life of the Holy Virgin Samthann: Medieval Hagiography, An Anthology*, Edited by Thomas F Head, New York, Routledge, 2001.

Saint Baldred (757 A.D.)

At your miracle well I will call to your soul
from a black yawning casket that Mercy will haul

And your elegant gannets would blanket the shoal
Like a halo your island would swell in their sprawl

You retreated to altar of granite and scroll
A true teacher plucks trappings from eyelids of all

On the Tyne there's an eddy renown as your whirl
What invaders struck down was a church, not its bell

From your roofless wild sanctum my prayer will unfurl
and it tremors with dreams only true love can tell

When your lantern dies out and my darknesses swirl
there the lightning will fly from the bright Micha-ël

Saint Baldred was a Gaelic monk and student of Saint Mungo. He evangelized what is now Lothian, Scotland. He set up a hermitage out on Bass Rock where he built a chapel. He ministered to the local villagers and performed miracles of healing. He was said to have walked on water, among many other spiritual comforts performed in preaching the gospel. He had a holy well and churches dedicated to him.

Micha-ël (Latin, Ecclesiastical): /mi.ka.el/ from the Hebrew meaning, "Who is like God?"[51]

---

51 O'Hanlon, Rev. John, *Lives of the Irish Saints*, Dublin, James Duffy and Sons, 1875.

Saint Aengus the Culdee (842 A.D.)

By the blankets of bog came a handwritten page
From scriptorium wrought by an angel and sage
In a grove by the stones where the willow tree sways
There a well gurgles swill where the seers engage
And from spirit and will speaks the Ancient of Days
For love's pail in the well fills the Ancient of Days

Over knolls of deep green rolls a river of trees
And a student of Fintan found oneness with these
For that hermit tamed self on the pitch of his play
Because rules of his game were angelic decrees
To be grateful to God who can quicken the clay
In that formless embrace of the quickening clay

 In the rose of my mind, in a God-smitten fling
I shall swim in an ovule that galaxies ring
And I'll sense beyond noise and detect beyond haze
That I've died in a desert that bursts in the Spring
In the beauty that rivals the angels ablaze
Where we thrive in Eternity, angels ablaze

A disciple of Mary was shown a great yew
And its limbs groped the sky, to forever they grew
Just as winds will erase the gray clouds in the way
Was there ever a tree that knew not what to do?

For the deed of the heart is to hold the born day
As a mother and child will unfold the born day

Aengus was born, educated by (St.) Fintan, lived and died, all at Clonenagh. After ordination he became an anchorite at nearby Disert Enos. So given to penance and prayer, the people called him the *Ceile Dei*, or Companion of God, anglicized, Culdee. With the abbot (St.) Maelruain (founder of the Ceile Dei movement), they collaborated to jointly compile *The Martyrology of Tallaght*. Later, his *Feilire* or *Festology of the Saints* (written in verse for easy remembering) appeared about 800 A.D. His *Book of Litanies* dates the invocation of the saints as a form of devotion in Ireland as early as the year 800. Aengus is thought to be the earliest of the writers on the Irish saints.[52]

---

52 D'Arcy, Mary, *The Saints of Ireland*, St. Paul, Irish American Cultural Institute, 1974.

Saint Baya and Saint Maura
(c. 9th Century)

They were two holy women we lost to that age
Where they talked about fog on the river of stars
There is no one to claim the same dusty abyss
As the silt on the sandbar reshuffles with tide

When they talked about fog on the river of stars
Was the island of Cumbrae repeating its sound?
When the silt on the sandbar reshuffles with tide
Sending verse to crustaceans emerged from the brine

Is the island of Cumbrae repeating its sound?
How the trees and the creatures still dialect God
Who sends verse to crustaceans emerged from the brine
On the shores where they slink and the waters
drink glow

How the trees and the creatures still dialect God
For two saints heard them chatting despite the
bright hush
On the shores where they slink and the waters
drink glow
The Eternal tends silos that someone must seal

For the saints hear them chatting despite the
bright hush

Of these two holy women we lost to that age
The Eternal tends silos that someone must seal
There is no one to claim the same dusty abyss

Saint Baya inhabited the island of Little Cumbrae, where she lived in solitude of nature. Saint Maura was friend to St. Baya and governed a community of ascetic nuns in Ayrshire, Scotland. Kilmaurs was a church dedicated to her. She would visit St Baya on her island for spiritual converse.[53]

53 Barrett, Dom Michael, *A Calendar of Scottish Saints*, Fort Augustus, The Abbey Press, 1919.

Author's Note

Ronnie Smith grew up in Chicago, Illinois and Baltimore, Maryland. He earned a bachelor's degree at Loyola University Maryland, and later studied engineering at the University of Maryland. Colonel Smith, retired from the Air Force after 30 years of service, where he commanded or flew over 1,000 flights in Antarctica. Challenged by extreme winds and temperatures that could drop to minus 75 degrees Fahrenheit during austral summer, physical and mental endurance were paramount to combat the rigors of prolonged operational stress. He discovered in that world contemplation and divine majesty. His poetry and paintings rest upon the foundation of the underlying wonder of God in humanity and creation. He looks forward to developing a spiritual retreat center in northern San Diego County where he resides. Its mission hopes to allow participants to reconnect to their own God-centered inner world, experienced in a sanctuary of the divine natural world.

~

If you have enjoyed reading this book, please post a review, long or short, on any book distributor sites (Amazon, Barnes and Noble, etc.). It is very appreciated and helps promote the work.

~

If you would like to place a bulk order for your parish, school, or friends, then please note that we offer special discounts on quantity purchases made by corporations, associations, schools, and others. For details or any comments, contact the author at:

Ronnie Smith/Plenus Gratia Publications
PlenusGratiaToday@gmail.com
www.PlenusGratia.com